HAPPINESS THROUGH TRANQUILLITY

The School of Epicurus

Richard W. Hibler

UNIVERSITY
PRESS OF
AMERICA

LANHAM • NEW YORK • LONDON

Copyright © 1984 by

University Press of America,™ Inc.

4720 Boston Way
Lanham, MD 20706

3 Henrietta Street
London WC2E 8LU England

Library of Congress Cataloging in Publication Data

Hibler, Richard W.
   Happiness through tranquility.

   Bibliography: p.
   1. Epicurus.   2. Philosophers—Greece—Biography.
3. Happiness.   I. Title.
B573.H53   1984   187   84-2324
ISBN 0-8191-3861-4 (alk. paper)
ISBN 0-8191-3862-2 (pbk. : alk. paper)

All University Press of America books are produced on acid-free
paper which exceeds the minimum standards set by the National
Historical Publications and Records Commission.

ACKNOWLEDGMENTS

The author wishes to thank the National Museum, Athens and the British Museum, London for assistance on this study. Special thanks are due to Professors Elsie Kristiansen, Arne Torp, P. G. Kouropies, A. M. Mylloyoja; artist-photographer Melon Grover; typist Eileen Loucks.

GENUS HUMANUM INGENIO SUPERAVIT,

ET OMNES PRAESTRINXIT,

STELLAS EXORTUS UTI AETHERIUS SOL.

HE [EPICURUS] WHOSE GENIUS

SURPASSED ALL HUMANKIND,

EXTINGUISHED THE LIGHT OF OTHERS,

AS THE STARS ARE DIMMED

BY THE RISING SUN.

LUCRETIUS
DE RERUM NATURA
BOOK 3, 1045

v

CONTENTS

PREFACE

This study examines some aspects of the life, teachings, and influence of the Hellenistic philosopher Epicurus. At the end of the fourth century and early part of the third century before Christ, the Greek teacher Epicurus converted disciples to his philosophy of happiness through tranquillity, and organized an educational system which significantly influenced the Hellenistic world and, later, Rome.

Academicians, Peripatetics, Stoics, Cynics, Skeptics, Cyrenaics, Rhetoricians, as well as Epicureans, vied for students in the ancient Mediterranean world. The influence of the Epicureans was immense, one need only read Plutarch, Cicero, and Seneca; the esteemed writers of the Roman world, to acknowledge the impact of the only philosopher in the ancient world to have a school named after him.

A founder or leader is usually identified with the Greek schools of philosophy. Plato is associated with the Academy, Aristotle is identified with the Lyceum, Zeno is the designated founder of Stoicism, Diogenes best represents the Cynics, Pyrrho is the most famous Skeptic, Isocrates developed a famed school of rhetoric, and Aristippus started the Cyrenaic School. Epicurus, alone among the philosophers, founded a school which adhered to his original tenets long after his death. Where each of the aforementioned schools redefined the message of the founder (Plato, Aristotle, Zeno, Aristippus) or most famous teacher (Diogenes, Pyrrho), the Epicureans never varied their philosophical religiosity to the commandments of Epicurus. This is why Epicurus is important. He gave direction and dimension to a school of thought which remained virtually unchanged for nearly eight hundred years.

Ralph Waldo Emerson, the proponent for self-reliance and individuality, once proclaimed that to be great is to be misunderstood. Emerson felt this was true of Pythagoras, Socrates, Jesus, and other nonconformists who offered new ideas only to receive abuse for their efforts. Perhaps more than any other ancient teacher, Epicurus has had to face the slings and arrows of outrageous distortion for his philosophy of egoistic hedonism. Even today, after years of scholarly research has acquitted him of charges of advocating licentious pleasure-seeking, the Epicurean to many is the prefiguration of vice. The fact that Epicurus' ideas have been grossly distorted can be attested by checking any dictionary. Webster's Unabridged Dictionary defines "epicurean" as "given to luxury or to sensual gratifications; adapted to luxurious tastes; luxurious." The Random House Dictionary defines "epicure" as "a person given up to sensual enjoyment."

In addition to the misuse of the term which carries his name, Epicurus must also bear the burden of anonymity and disregard in the field of educational history and philosophy. Most publications in the field of educational foundations give little or no mention of Epicurus and his school. Compared to the Academy of Plato, which is subject to intense investigation by educational historians (often necessitating a separate chapter in a history or philosophy book), the Garden School of Epicurus is mentioned, if at all, only in passing. A truer assessment of the value of Epicurus to history is found in <u>The Faith of Epicurus</u> by the noted classical scholar Benjamin Farrington, Emeritus Professor of Classics at the University College of Swansea.

> ... What is certain is that the sayings of
> Epicurus, as they are, represent a protest
> from a man of different temperament,
> sensibility, and aims; and that they cut so
> deep and proved so effective that Epicureanism,
> rightly judged, is found to be an historical
> phenomenon as important as Platonism.[1]

Educational historians and philosophers often suggest that history repeats itself, or runs in cycles. Practices and policies common to the past may appear over and over again. If we accept this supposition, and the consequences it presents for education, the present and future of the profession can be helped by a reflective look at the experience of the past. A school which significantly influenced the structure of civilization in ancient Greece and Rome is the Garden School of Epicurus. Since the great civilizations of the Mediterranean influenced all subsequent world history, including the educational foundations of present Western society, a study of Epicurus and his school will contribute to a better understanding of the present educational culture.

An historical account of Epicurus reveals an amiable, intelligent, and dedicated educator offering, through the example of his life and teachings, a guide for human behavior. An historical perspective may inspire introspective reflection and a subsequent change of behavior on the part of students and teachers reading about the philosopher-educator and his ideas. If, on the other hand, knowledge of the life and philosophical doctrines of Epicurus does not contribute to increased professional competency, a reader will still profit from the entertainment value of an enriched understanding of the salient features of a significant school of ancient educational thought.

Finally, the purpose of this study is not to examine the metaphysical, epistemological, or axiological underpinings of Epicurean philosophy. Reference is made to the three philosophical branches only when applicable as elucidation for a description of Epicurus' school and theory of education. Detailed explanation of metaphysics, epistemology, and axiology will be found in several of the books listed under **SELECTED REFERENCES**.

Since previous scholarship has covered the field of Epicurean philosophic research, this study limits its investigation to the most important features of an Epicurean pedagogical system. Where the cosmology, ontology, and other speculative features concerning the nature of the universe and physical properties, with special attention to Epicurean atomistic theory, have characterized other writings, this study explores the nature of Epicurus as a teacher and educational theorist.

EPICURUS

HERMARCHUS

CHAPTER I

EPICURUS THE TEACHER

Across the Aegean Sea from the mainland of Greece, just two miles offshore from Turkey, is the mountainous island of Samos. This forested and fertile island has been noted since antiquity for the fine quality of its wines. Herodotus, the historian of the Greek and Persian wars, had a special fondness for Samos and its inhabitants, stating that he admired the people because three of the greatest engineering feats in history were accomplished by them. First was a nearly one mile tunnel under a mountain, the second engineering marvel was a four hundred yard breakwater around the harbor, and third was a gigantic temple built in honor of Hera. Parts of each of these may be seen today on Samos.

On this island Epicurus, son of Neocles, was born in February, 341 B.C. His father, from an old Athenian family, moved to Samos a few years before the future philosopher was born. Neocles, an immigrant because of economic necessity, joined other Athenian colonists and founded a transplanted home across the Aegean from the mainland. Because he was the son of a poor school teacher born far away from Athens, Epicurus was subjected to the taunts of later critics about his low birth among the provincial rustics (Athenian-bred Greeks always felt themselves superior to other Greeks).

Not only was his island birth looked upon as

1

inferior to birth on the mainland, but Neocles, a poor man, gave Epicurus low social status in the eyes of a class-conscious society. While Plato was an aristocrat from the family of Solon; Aristotle, son of a court physician in Macedonia, Epicurus was an elementary school teacher's son! To understand the indignity of being a school teacher in ancient Greece, one must remember that they were respected little more than women and slaves, who, like the teachers, spent most of their time with children and were not thought fit company for men.

In addition to assisting his father in school, the future philosopher is reported to have helped his mother in a most unusual occupation. From an early age Epicurus was required to follow his mother, Chaerestrata, to peasant houses and assist her with fortune-telling. Chaerestrata performed certain shamanistic folk rituals which the peasants believed would aid crop growth, insure health for the family, and avert natural disasters. In a region where calamity could strike through the caprice of a god in the form of earthquake, drought, and other horrors, the peasants often relied on religious and magical rites for insurance. In later life Epicurus would become a spokesman for the most rigid denunciation of superstition. Perhaps the basis for his mature philosophy of rejecting all myths and stories of supernatural intervention in human lives may be traced to the experiences of his youth when he served as a sorceress's apprentice.

Epicurus shared a happy childhood with his three brothers: Neocles, Chaeredemus, and Aristobulus; he was a dutiful son and remained devoted to his parents. The family remained close and each of his brothers joined the philosopher in Athens after he had established his school. Around the age of twelve Epicurus began to study philosophy, an indication he had an inquiring mind and facile intelligence at an early age.

At age eighteen, along with all other youth of Athenian citizenship - regardless of home - Epicurus left Samos for two years military duty in Athens. In the same year Alexander (the Great) of Macedon died, 323 B.C., the future philosopher arrived to begin his cadetship. Athens with its two great schools, the Academy and the Lyceum; with Dionysiac festivals, theatre, musical contests,

2

and athletic events must have appeared as a surprising contrast to the quiet life on the small agricultural island of Samos. To share the excitement of the city Epicurus established friendship with a fellow cadet, Menander, destined to become the most famous dramatist of his day. Although Epicurus was a year older than his companion-at-arms, they served together in the garrison and shared many ideas. There is no doubt that the cadet from Samos exerted an influence on the future playwright. In his writing Menander makes no direct reference to Epicurus, but scholars have suggested that many doctrines from the philosopher were adapted for their dramatic possibilities.

For ten years following his military service in Athens Epicurus lived with his family in Colophon. The move to Colophon by his parents was necessary because in 322 B.C. a dictator expelled the Athenian colonists from Samos. Little is known about this period of his life, but there is no question it was a time for study, reflection, and the development of philosophic insight. As Colophon, on the mainland of Asia Minor near Ephesus, offered little opportunity for advanced study, it is likely that Epicurus traveled to Rhodes and other intellectual centers to study with a variety of teachers. Also during this period the young philosopher was cultivating his own independent educational ideas, later to be incorporated into Epicurean philosophy.

Around the age thirty Epicurus felt confident of his own pedagogical skills and moved to Mytilene on the island of Lesbos to begin teaching. This was a famous educational center, Aristotle had taught on the island years before and left an influential Peripatetic school. Epicurus, flushed with the enthusiasm of his own burgeoning philosophy, immediately came into conflict with the followers of Plato and Aristotle. Because he spent time in Mytilene belittling the philosophical efforts of his fellow teachers Epicurus made enemies, but he also gained converts to his philosophy. One was Hermarchus, who spent the rest of his life with the philosopher and after the death of Epicurus became head of the Athenian school.

After a short stay Epicurus, now joined by his new friend Hermarchus, had to leave Mytilene because of the hostility of the influential Academicians and Peripatetics. They moved to

3

Lampsacus on the Hellespont for a period of four years between 310 and 306 B.C. This was one of the most successful periods of Epicurus' teaching because in the city on the Dardanelles he made the most important philosophical converts of his life. Names which appear over and over in his correspondence (and in his last will and testament forty years later) became devoted disciples to the philosopher. Included was his closest friend and associate, Metrodorus; as well as Idomeneus, Colotes, Polyaneus, Pythocles, Leonteus, and Themista. These were men and women of position and influence without whose moral encouragement and financial resources Epicurus would have found difficulty in establishing his school in Athens. Finally in 306 B. C., at the age of thirty-five, Epicurus with several of his friends left Lampsacus to take up residence in Athens.

ATHENS AND EPICURUS' GARDEN SCHOOL

Today the site of Plato's Academy is located in northwest Athens about a mile from the Agora in the Valley of Kephissos. During the life of Plato, and for generations thereafter, it was a beautiful grove of plane, elm, and olive trees bordered by shady walks. Today, however, a residential area has swallowed all semblance to the past and only a few scattered archaeological sites (including the foundation for the Academy gymnasium and peristyle peripatos) remind the visitor that this was the site of Plato's famous school.

Along the road to the Academy, perhaps half-way between Plato's grove and the Athenian Agora (near what is today the Church of St. George) was Epicurus' Garden School. A maze of tenement houses, congested streets, and small businesses make it impossible in the present day to envision the site 2000 years ago. Two hundred years after Epicurus' death Cicero with his Epicurean friend Pomponius visited the Garden on their way to Plato's Academy. Unfortunately, Cicero gave only a general and inadequate description of his visit and this is the only written record of the approximate location of Epicurus' school.

Epicurus purchased his Garden for a small sum and then bought a house some distance away in a

4

section of town, located between the Acropolis and Piraeus, called Melite. The Garden, unlike Plato's Academy which was located in a large park, was quite small. The school was called the Garden because the resident-members provided for their own food, growing a variety of vegetables including lettuce, cabbages, onions, cucumbers, celery and many herbs and spices. It is not surprising that members of the school provided for their own food, because self-sufficiency was a keynote of the Epicurean living pattern and by growing their own vegetables the students and teachers were guarding against the possibility of food shortage during troubled times. In fact, their precautions were wisely taken because during the political power struggles of Demetrius Poliorcetes, in the early years of the third century B.C., military campaigns in and around Athens caused hardship and hunger among the residents.

While students lived at the Garden, philosophizing among the onions and cucumbers, the house of Epicurus in Melite served another purpose. It was a small building according to Cicero, yet its function was more than a residence for the leader of the school. It served as a publishing house for the extensive writing done by Epicurus and his disciples. Students in the house copied manuscripts and arranged for the distribution of Epicurean writing to followers living throughout the Greek world.

The Garden, and house at Melite, as well as Aristotle's Lyceum, Zeno's Painted Stoa, and Plato's Academy are buried beneath a modern and rapidly growing city of four million inhabitants. Surprisingly, some of the haunting grandeur of ancient Athens remains in the metropolis today to awaken the visitor's imagination of what the architecture was like 2300 years ago.

PHYSICAL FEATURES AND HEALTH OF EPICURUS

Until his death at the age of seventy, Epicurus lived with his students and friends on the outskirts of Athens. It was during his long tenure in the city that the philosopher from Samos acquired the name which his students and followers would reverentially use throughout antiquity - they would simply call him "Master." The life style of the

5

Master and disciples can be surmised by a wealth of evidence from his own works, those of friends, and the comments from his critics and enemies. For instance, it is known how Epicurus looked because a number of statues remain which give an accurate portrayal of his appearance.

In museums throughout the world (particularly in Rome, Naples, and London) are original sculptures which portray the strength of character and strong personality of the ancient educator. All statues, plus statuettes and a few engraved gems from the Roman period, show the striking physical features of the Master. He had a long, narrow head with a deeply-lined high forehead. The eyes were small, with drooping upper lids and pockets beneath the lower lids; the nose was very long with a marked protuberance below the bridge. Epicurus, like nearly all ancient philosophers, wore a long full beard. Unlike Socrates, Plato, Antisthenes, and other philosophers identified by portrait or sculpture who possessed round full faces, the philosopher of the Garden was thin.

One reason Epicurus was lean, in fact gaunt in appearance, was because of his delicate health. Evidence from Suidas, Laertius, Aelian, and Plutarch that the Master was never physically strong, leads some scholars to suggest Epicurus used a forerunner of today's wheelchair to travel around Athens. There is a strong likelihood this was true because the philosopher suffered from a stone in his bladder or kidneys and such an infirmity would have caused pain and discomfort in walking. Epicurus braved his disability with a fortitude which was respected by all commentators, even his philosophical detractors.

In 270 B.C. the Master died from the ailment in his bladder or kidneys. He faced death with such remarkable courage that his forbearance in the face of pain was proverbial throughout the ancient world. Cicero, who had Stoic sympathies and wrote some of the most inflammatory condemnations of Epicurean philosophy, marveled at the personal bravery shown by the dying philosopher. In De Finibus, Cicero ranked the death scene of Epicurus on a level with those of Epaminondas and Leonidas, two Greek generals who died bravely on the battlefield.

Cicero also suggested - and this is unusual

6

considering the pain the Master was experiencing - that Epicurus was happy on the brink of death. Such a claim is supported by a letter which the dying man wrote to a faithful disciple, Idomeneus; the contents offer an impressive picture of the personality of the philosopher.

> On this truly happy day of my life, as I am at the
> point of death, I write this to you. The disease in
> my bladder and stomach is pursuing its course,
> lacking nothing of its natural severity: but against
> all this is the joy in my heart at the recollection
> of my conversations with you.[1]

How can a dying man with a painful inflammation be happy? The answer is found in the words of Epicurus and in the tenets of his philosophy. From the preserved writings of the Master the following epigrams exhibit the contempt for death on one hand and the Epicurean joy of living on the other hand, which characterized the leader of the Garden during his last days.

> On the journey of life we must try to make the end
> better than the beginning, as long as we are en route;
> but when we come to the journey's end, we must be
> cheerful and tranquil.[2]

> We should not think of a young man as being happy,
> but rather the old man who has lived a good life.
> The young man at the height of his power is change-
> able and carried from his course by fortune, like a
> meandering river. But the old man has come to
> anchor in old age as though in mooring, and holds
> in his thankful memory all the blessings for which
> he could once barely hope.[3]

> When it is time for us to depart, derisively spitting
> upon life and those who vainly cling to it, we shall
> leave this life singing aloud the victory anthem that
> we have lived a good life.[4]

The second quotation, which describes the old man in blissful happiness during his last days, is similar to an expression by Seneca, the Roman essayist, who said that since man lives his life on the high seas, he should die in harbor. Compared with the passivity of spirit in quotation number two is a contrasting fervor and evangelical zeal in the third quotation. Although the wording in each differs, all three pronouncements share a similar

7

Epicurean theme which was a plea to live in peace of mind, appreciation of life, and a refusal to fear death. The idea that "death has no sting" and should be met with a serene mind is central to Epicurean philosophy. The most famous disciple of the Master (albeit he lived several centuries later) was the Roman poet Titus Lucretius Carus who wrote De Rerum Natura (On the Nature of Things). Lucretius, like his teacher Epicurus, was very dogmatic about the death theory central to the Garden philosophy. In his great poetic work the Roman Epicurean mentions that death has no meaning, it is totally irrelevant to the conditions of life; since the mind of mortal man should forget about death altogether. Lucretius also preaches a refrain similar to Epicurus and Seneca when he compares death to sleep, where the soul is at rest; at mooring on quiet seas where it can never be disturbed.

Epicurus lived and died happy, even while suffering from a crippling and painful disease. He did not fear death because he had no fear of the afterlife, rather his energies were devoted to finding peace of mind and contentment on earth. It was this attitude, rejecting the concept of the immortal soul, which led to charges of impiety and even atheism from his critics. Many detractors faulted his philosophy, especially concerning the topic of immortality of the soul because this was central to the thesis of the Platonists; but few during his lifetime insulted and demeaned the character and life style of Epicurus as a man.

CRITICISMS OF THE MASTER

One of those who did vilify the philosopher was a man who knew him well. A former student and friend, Timocrates, brother of Epicurus' closest friend Metrodorus, left the school of Athens and began a campaign of scurrilous gossip. Diogenes Laertius, who discounted the insults as complete fabrications - even to calling Timocrates "stark mad" - reports the following from the Master's ex-disciple.

He in the book entitled Merriment asserts that
Epicurus vomited twice a day from over-indulgence,
and goes on to say that he himself had much ado

8

to escape from those notorious midnight philoso-
phizings and the confraternity with all its secrets;
further that Epicurus's acquaintance with philosophy
was small and his acquaintance with life even smaller;
that his bodily health was pitiful. . . .[5]

Such a range of charges and innuendoes appear
quite severe. However, most scholars have dismissed
the suggestion that Timocrates was accurate in his
appraisal of the life and conduct of the philosopher
from Samos. Timocrates was likely jealous of the
warm friendship between his brother Metrodorus and
Epicurus, and it has been suggested that he was
upset with Epicurus for assigning him to a teaching
position in an undesirable location. In addition,
the statement of Timocrates must be discounted because
all evidence points to an entirely different character
for Epicurus than the one described in Merriment.
An examination of the life style, personal habits,
and character of the Master reveal exactly the
opposite from the report by Metrodorus' brother.

Life Style, Habits, and Character of an Ascetic

Timocrates wrote the first authenticated
condemnation of the Garden philosopher, defaming
his reputation, and charging the Master with sybaritic
pleasure pursuits. Not surprisingly, considering
the hedonistic philosophy he advocated, Epicurus
found other critics who misunderstood his teachings;
subjected his name to calumny and helped develop
the myth of Epicureanism as a life style given to
sensual gratifications. As a result of criticism
throughout Greek and Roman antiquity dictionaries
today define small-e, epicurean, as a person with
luxurious, carnal, or self-indulgent tastes. Nothing
could be further from the true definition of big-E,
Epicureanism, than small-e, epicureanism!

Diogenes Laertius, a Roman scholar in the late
second or early third century A.D., wrote much of
what we know about the Master in Lives and Opinions
of the Famous Philosophers, in which he describes
in some detail the life style of the controversial
teacher. In regard to eating habits, Laertius
suggests that Epicurus was content with plain bread
and water; only occasionally varying the diet when
he would add a little cheese and, perhaps, some

vegetables from his garden. This - certainly - does not sound like the self-indulgent sensuality the word epicure brings to mind!

Even the proud and frugal Stoics acknowledged the refined character of Epicurus. The Roman Seneca, who unsuccessfully attempted to tutor the reprobate Nero, wrote letters and essays on Stoic philosophy and used the Master as a model of propriety. In one letter to Lucilius, Seneca describes the Garden School of Epicurus and recounts the pleasures of forebearance:

> Go to his Garden and read the motto carved there: 'Stranger, here you will do well to tarry; here our highest good is pleasure.' The caretaker of that abode, a kindly host, will be ready for you; he will welcome you with barley-meal and serve you water also in abundance, with these words: 'Have you not been well entertained?' 'This garden,' he says, 'does not whet your appetite; it quenches it.'[6]

In an earlier letter Seneca suggests that barley bread and water, although not a sumptuous diet, can offer the highest degree of pleasure because a rich banquet is not necessary for happiness.

Many have agreed with this proposition, Diogenes the Cynic, for example, is quoted as saying that he would rather live on a few grains of salt at home in Athens than share in a luxurious dinner at Craterus' table. Certainly no one would accuse Diogenes or Seneca of advocating and following sensual, hedonistic pursuits. However, Epicurus has been called a sensual hedonist for 2300 years, and yet - he was the originator of the "bread and water" theorem of eating! As the Master dogmatically stated: "I find full pleasure in the body when I live on bread and water, and I spit upon the pleasures of plush living not for their own account, but because of the discomforts that follow them."[7]

Not only was the ascetic Greek teacher opposed to sumptuous feasts, all the "pleasures of plush living" were an anathema to him. One of his famous epigrams states: "It is better for you to lie upon a bed of straw and be free of fear, than to have a golden couch and an opulent table, yet be troubled in mind."[8] There is a portion of Seneca's Moral Essays which copies almost to the word the sentiment of Epicurus. The Stoic mentions that he can be

10

just as happy on a handful of hay as resting on a soft mattress with purple (the color of nobility) coverings. It is little wonder that Seneca, who shared so many ascetic ideas with Epicurus, would find the character and quiet life style of the Greek philosopher worthy of commendation.

The teacher from Samos does not sound like the base and ugly sensualist which Timocrates painted him. In fact, his conduct was more suggestive of a saint; and when comparing the Master to a saint it must be noted he followed the rules of poverty, chastity, and obedience. Poverty was a condition often present at the Garden because Epicurus and his students had, literally, to divide a ration of beans among themselves during meal time. The Master followed the rule of chastity by never marrying and, in probability, by never having sexual relations. Epicurus' attitude toward sex is expressed with saintly fervor in an apothegm addressed to his students where he exhorts them to forego sexual relations, because such practices never contribute to improving man's condition and often lead to serious harm. Finally, the last point on the route to sainthood was obedience to his own philosophical doctrines, which was such a distinguishing feature of the Garden teacher that his associates proclaimed the Master as "living proof" of their way of life.

Therefore, it can be stated with evidential authority that Epicurus did not lead a corrupt, dissolute life devoted to sybaritic pleasures. Rather, the facts confirm that the Greek teacher was, indeed, in life style, habit, and character a true ascetic.

EPICURUS, TEACHER IN THE GARDEN SCHOOL

Except for two or three brief periods when he visited Aegean islands, Epicurus never left his Garden School in Athens. For half of his seventy years he sequestered himself with friends and relatives in his own private grove of Academe.

One ancient source offers a comprehensive description of the organization of Epicurus' school. In Seneca's Moral Letters is a clear indication of the interrelationships and responsibilities between teachers and students. It was a hierarchical

11

structure with Epicurus as the leader on top of a pyramid of authority. In an arrangement reminiscent of the organization of Plato's three levels of learning: guardians (philosopher-kings), auxiliaries (soldiers), and artisans (workers); Epicurus divided his teaching and learning teams into different levels. In this system there were some, Epicurus said, who became wise by working out their own way to the truth, needing no assistance from others. Obviously, as the originator and independent thinker who developed the tenets of his own philosophy, he represented this top category as leader. The Master never doubted for a moment that he was an independent truthseeker, although the point has been cause for serious debate for 2300 years. Many authorities believe Epicurus was not an originator of an independent system of philosophy, but rather synthesized the atomism and ethics of previous writers and teachers.

The Garden leader was so convinced of the righteousness and truth of his endeavors he required total obedience to his dictums and educational system. For this reason a motto was popular at the school which stated: "Cherish some man of high character, and keep him ever before your eyes, living as if he were watching you, and ordering all your actions as if he beheld them."[9] It was obvious to other teachers at the Garden School, as well as to all the students, who the model for high character should be - Epicurus. If a slow learner could not catch the hint from the previous motto, another more succinct and specific slogan was used: "Do all things as if Epicurus were looking at you."[10] This appears to be a rather dictatorial attitude (some might claim it was megalomaniacal) but, in point of fact, Epicurus was a gentle and benevolent dictator-leader. When the crippled philosopher from Samos was called "Master" or "Leader" it was from reverential respect and love, not fear, that provided him complete authority at the school.

Next to Epicurus in the line of authority were those who needed someone else to lead while they followed obediently. Three men: Metrodorus, Hermarchus, and Polyaenus served as "associate leaders," and it was understood that they followed in the footsteps of the Master although each was capable of teaching the Epicurean dogma.

Cicero mentions Metrodorus as a person who

was a twin of Epicurus. This was not to suggest that Cicero believed they looked alike because sculpture portraits of Metrodorus do not resemble the Master, but rather the Roman writer was suggesting that both men thought alike. Rarely have two philosophers shared such a deep respect and friendship for one another. Diogenes Laertius mentions numerous incidents where each man showed affection for the other: Metrodorus named one of his sons for Epicurus and, in his will, the head of the Garden School made provision for Metrodorus' children. Epicurus in his writings mentioned his friend many times and in each instance deeply praised the goodness, sincerity, and serenity of Metrodorus' character. Metrodorus, like other leaders of the Garden, wrote a number of books, but only a few fragments remain today. However, some of the titles have been preserved, among them: Epicurus' Weak Health, The Way to Wisdom, and Of Noble Birth (the last named was a defense of Epicurus). Metrodorus at age fifty-three died seven years before the Master.

The memory of Metrodorus was retained with reverent affection by following generations of Epicureans. In his will, Epicurus advised his followers to perpetuate the memory of Metrodorus and himself with special commemorative celebrations to be held on the twentieth day of each month. Metrodorus and Hermarchus, as Epicurus' closest associates, were popular sculpture subjects during Roman times; Metrodorus' portrait on a famous double herm with Epicurus (in the Capitoline Museum in Rome) shows the face of a serene philosopher who followed the tenets of the Master's philosophy of tranquillity.

Hermarchus superseded Epicurus as leader of the Garden, however, he probably did not serve very long, because he was at least seventy years old when he became the second head of the School. Hermarchus, according to Diogenes Laertius, was the son of a poor man and he was a student of rhetoric when he met Epicurus in Mytilene around 312 B.C. Like Metrodorus, Hermarchus followed his leader to Athens in 306 B.C. and remained there the rest of his life.

The intellectual reputation of Epicurus' school was enhanced during its formative stages by the addition of the famed mathematician Polyaenus, a citizen of Lampsacus. Epicurus needed two factors

13

to aid him in establishing a competitive position
for his school in Athens. One requisite for success
was enough money to function; this was provided
by friends such as Leonteus and Themista. The second
urgent need, as for any ancient Athenian school
hoping to attract students, was a scholar of
reputation. In the Garden, Polyaenus was this man.
Little is known about the mathematician other than
his reputation as a kind, honest, and dependable
teacher.

ASSISTANT LEADERS IN THE GARDEN SCHOOL

Beneath the "Associate Leaders" in Epicurus'
school were "Assistant Leaders." Names of the
assistant leaders are not known, but conjecture
offers striking possibilities. For instance, a
woman, Leontion, mentioned by several ancient sources
as the wife (or concubine-companion) of Metrodorus,
studied at the school and became renowned as a
scholar. This is of inestimable importance because
it suggests that the Epicurean school was the first
in history to provide an instructional and leadership
position to a woman. Plato, as is well known, made
provision for female students and advocated equality
for women; at least two, Lastheneia of Mantinea
and Axiothea of Phlius (who wore men's clothes),
attended his Academy. However, neither assumed
a leadership role in the Academy, and history does
not record any scholarly achievements for Lastheneia
or Axiothea.

It is likely Leontion held a leadership position
in the Garden because she wrote treatises in defense
of Epicurus and earned an academic reputation
throughout the Greek world. This is remarkable
considering her career before joining the
philosophical school - she was an hetaira or
professional courtesan. A number of ancient Greek
hetairai gained fame through their association with
famous statesmen, philosophers, and artists.
Leontion, in association with Epicurus, joined other
courtesans who were friends and lovers of noted
personalities, such as: Lais, associated with the
philosophers Aristippus and Diogenes; Phryne, friend
of Hypereides the orator and Praxiteles the artist.
Of course, the most famous hetaira was Aspasia,
who was consort to the illustrious statesman Pericles

14

during the "Golden Age" of Greece in the fifth century B.C.

It appears there were other hetairai at the Garden School in addition to Leontion, because scholars have found names such as Hedia ("Sweetie"), Erotion ("Lovey"), among the women living at the Garden. Likely such names were used before they came to Epicurus' school and, although they renounced the profession of prostitution when they joined the philosophers, they evidently kept their nicknames. The communal life of the Garden with former hetairai in attendance led to charges of promiscuity by Epicurean critics. However, closer examination of life at the school would have enlightened detractors, because Epicurus specifically discouraged sexual relations.

If, as it appears probable, Leontion was indeed an assistant leader in the Garden, she would have been joined by several men (perhaps Epicurus' brothers were among them) to give most of the public and private lectures at the school. Except for the most advanced, students received their direct instruction from the assistant leaders.

It is known that teachers and students, male and female - young and old - lived together at the school, because in his will Epicurus provided for "fellow-members" to live in his house and study at the Garden. Most were probably impecunious, as was certainly true of Epicurus' slave Mys, who was a student. Mys, along with other slaves who were fellow-members, offer, along with the women, another contrast between the Epicurean school and other philosophical institutions in ancient Greece. Scholars generally believe the Garden of Epicurus was the only major school of philosophy in Greece to admit slaves.

VENERATION FOR EPICURUS

A fragment remains from a letter Epicurus sent to his student Colotes which offers insight into the veneration and high regard in which he was held by students.

> In your feeling of reverence for what I was then
> saying you were seized with an unaccountable
> desire to embrace me and clasp my knees and
> show me all the signs of homage paid by men in
> prayers and supplications to others; so you made
> me return all these proofs of veneration and
> respect to you.[11]

The action of prostrate, or perhaps it was kneeling, homage shown to Epicurus by Colotes was very unusual. The ancient Greeks, except when forced by a tyrant (as in the case of Alexander of Macedon), did not offer obeisance to living men. Most Greeks believed a gesture of deference was a barbarian trait to be associated with Persian Kings. In fact, it was from his experience in Persia and the Near East that Alexander may have developed his neurotic idea about his personal divine ordination, thereby, demanding veneration from his associates.

Plutarch, rather sardonically, describes Colotes' action and mentions the Master returning the heart-felt gesture of his disciple by worshipful praise. Epicurus demanded respect because he was the leader, the Master of the Garden. During his lifetime and for centuries thereafter, students of Epicurean philosophy would acknowledge the Hellenistic philosopher as a god-head. It is very doubtful whether he wanted, and certainly he did not demand, this kind of adulation. Epicurus, from all accounts, was not humble and self-effacing, but he was equally not imperious and consumed by delusions of grandeur. To his followers, however, Epicurus was a savior and they showed their appreciation in many ways.

The most famous expression of devotion in this regard belongs to Lucretius. One cannot read the Roman poet without picturing him in a literary swoon over his hero. Although several portions of De Rerum Natura are devoted to ecstatic verse in praise of the Greek teacher, one excerpt from Book III will serve as an example of Lucretius' consecration to the memory of Epicurus.

> Then, who from out of the darkness
> Raised a torch aloft to shed light
> Upon the blessings of life;
> I follow thee, brightest star of the Greeks. . . .
> How can a swallow contend with the swan?

16

In a test of speed can little goats hope
To match the wobbly strength of their spindly legs
Against the power and quickness of the great steed?[12]

Such an effusive description appears humorous in some ways. For instance, comparing the Greek philosopher to a great steed in "power and quickness" is certainly an awkward analogy considering the fact that Epicurus, weak in health, lived in a wheelchair!

Another humorous tribute to Epicurus was paid by the famous Roman Pompenius, later known, because of his affection for Greece (Attica), as Atticus. Pompenius was a close friend of Cicero and was constantly on the defense protecting the reputation of Epicureanism from the smears and insults of Stoics. Once accused of always bringing forth the name of Epicurus, Pompenius retorted:

Still I could not forget Epicurus, even if I
wanted; the members of our body not only
have pictures of him, but even have his
likeness on their drinking-cups and rings.[13]

In the British Museum, London are two jewelled relics representing a profile of Epicurus. One is a red jasper engraved gem from the Blacas Collection; the other a gem on a plasm in the Carlisle Collection. Gems bearing a likeness of the philosopher are also on display in the National Museum, Naples. Epicurus was such a divinity to his followers that many had pictures of him in their homes and they wore rings carved in his likeness.

The pictures, sculptures, rings, and engraved gems bearing the face of Epicurus, and used by his followers during Greek and Roman times, are similar to the popularity of the images of religious leaders, such as Jesus and the Buddha. In the same way that pictures of Christ and the Buddha are found in homes and churches throughout the world, Epicurus' face was found decorating monuments in the ancient world.

HOLY DAYS AND CELEBRATIONS OF THE TWENTYERS

In his last will, the Master commanded that his followers meet for the celebration of his birthday

17

on the tenth day of Gamelion (February) in each
year, and to hold a special meeting each month on
the twentieth day to commemorate Metrodorus and
himself. Cicero speaks about a sum of money provided
on the twentieth day of each month for the followers
of the Master to honor his memory by a banquet.
Scholars are in agreement that the twentieth day
of the month served as a feast day; perhaps the
ascetic Epicureans ate a little cheese in
commemoration of Epicurus' suggestion that he would
eat "a little pot of cheese" when he wished to feast
sumptuously. The Epicurean celebration of the
twentieth was not an orgy; hedonists like the ex-slave
Trimalchio in Petronius' Satyricon would have been
very disappointed in the menu. The dinner date
must have involved philosophical discussion and
perhaps eulogistic oratory. Whatever the case,
twelve books - now lost - called the Arguments of
Diocles were written about the celebrations,
unquestionably a sign that ritual and philosophical
custom followed a liturgical pattern.

The date, the twentieth of the month, was an
interesting choice by Epicurus. For that was a
sacred day to the celebrants of Apollo at Delphi
and it was also the day on which initiation rites
were held at the Temple of Demeter in Eleusis. In
derision, the enemies of the Master named his cult
Eikadistai which is from the Greek word for the
twentieth (Eikas), and therefore forms the word
for Men of the Twentieth. In the same way that
followers of Christ in Roman times were ridiculed
with the name "Christian," eventually the members
of the Epicurean and Christian faiths accepted their
respective new names and became proud of them.

CHAPTER II

THE EPICUREAN PHILOSOPHY OF HAPPINESS

Lucretius' De Rerum Natura (The Nature of Things), as a literary classic, follows a most improbable theme. It is a poetic exposition of Epicurean philosophy with an emphasis on the atomistic and materialistic state of the cosmos. Epistemological and axiological ideas are developed in the poem, but the emphasis is clearly upon answering metaphysical questions about the nature of reality. Apparently Lucretius, the dutiful student to Epicurus, felt scientific explanations to physical conditions were of extreme importance in developing the philosophical system of the Garden. Therefore, long passages of the Latin poem deal with the postulates of atomism, Epicurus' atomic-swerve theory, and a pseudo-scientific look at meteorology, earthquakes, volcanoes, and other physical phenomena.

Lucretius borrowed his ideas from the teachings of Epicurus and writings from the Athenian Garden School, but unfortunately, the "scientific" data were not always accurate. In one poetic stanza Lucretius suggests the reason the Nile River floods in summer is because northern winds blow with such force that the water is forced over its banks. There are dozens of examples of explanations for physical phenomena in De Rerum Natura which small children today would know to be false. Ironically, Epicurean answers to scientific questions sometimes held a truth which was not experimentally proven until centuries later. For instance Book IV in Lucretius'

19

epic hypothesizes on smells, reaching conclusions which scientists only recently accepted.

In addition to Lucretius, two of the three extant letters written by Epicurus, the <u>Letter to Herodotus</u> and the <u>Letter to Pythocles</u>, deal with scientific information. The Roman poet evidently received much of his information from these two sources because the subject matter in the letters and in the poem are identical. In the <u>Letter to Herodotus</u>, Epicurus lectures on the facts of sense-perception, atoms, the soul, cosmology, meteorology, and celestial phenomena; plus an outline of the growth of civilization and origin of language. The letter is only thirteen pages long so it is readily apparent that the Greek teacher summarized his subject. His books on physical science doubtless provided a detailed analysis of each scientific area, however, those works have been lost.

The <u>Letter to Pythocles</u> is only nine pages long and there is some question as to its authenticity. When comparing it to the other letters (<u>Herodotus</u> and <u>Menoeceus</u>), noteworthy differences appear in syntax and content. Whatever the origin; written by Epicurus, by one of his pupils, or an abridged compilation by a number of writers, the source is definitely Epicurean and the contents are similar to Lucretius' Book VI of <u>De Rerum Natura</u>. The <u>Letter to Pythocles</u> mentions heavenly phenomena; atmospheric and meteorological conditions such as clouds, thunder, snow, rainbows, and even weather forecasting. Unfortunately, Epicurus' scientific ignorance provided some humorous answers to the question of the origin of physical phenomena. The following are a number of examples from his conclusions about physical science.

> Earthquakes may be produced when wind is shut up in the earth, divided alongside of small masses of earth, and continuously shaken, causing the earth to quiver.[1]

> The size of the sun and moon and the other celestial bodies is, for us, such as it seems to be. In reality, it is a little greater than we see it or a little less or about the same. . . .[2]

> A thunderbolt **may be** formed when, after many eddies of wind are crowded together and have burst violently into flame, a part of the fire breaks

out and falls with even greater violence on
the places below.[3]

Perhaps the aforementioned "facts" are not a fair
representation of Epicurean study into natural
phenomena, indeed, most of the scientific conclusions
were quite accurate. Certainly the atomic theory
which Epicurus borrowed from the pre-Socratics,
Leucippus and Democritus, was 2000 years ahead of
its time.

The most significant feature of all Epicurean
work in scientific investigation is the fact that
the conclusions that the Master and his followers
reached about physical phenomena was not, in and
of itself, important. Epicurus was not a scientist
and had nothing but disdain for pure scientific
inquiry! Amazingly, he was not really concerned
whether his scientific hypotheses were provable
by experimentation.

FREEDOM FROM FEAR AND MENTAL UNCERTAINTY

An examination of the letters to Herodotus
and Pythocles give an immediate indication that
the Master was not attempting to duplicate the
voluminous investigative fields of Aristotle. Quite
the contrary, Epicurus narrowed his inquiry to
problems where people needed answers to questions
that caused them fear. All of his scientific reports
were in areas where the populace of ancient times
worried about the intervention of gods and
supernatural causations in the physical realm. It
was Epicurus' purpose not to provide accurate
scientific data for the world of scholarship, but
rather to alleviate fears about the unknown. This
was the reason the Greek teacher prefaced all of
his writing with the injunction that the aim of
knowledge is freedom from fear and mental uncertainty.
In his Letter to Pythocles, the reason for his
scientific investigation into the heavenly phenomena
is clearly explained as the attempt to gain knowledge
to provide peace of mind.

To develop the self-confidence of his students
where they would have no fear of the cosmic unknown,
Epicurus parted company with previous philosophers,

21

especially the Socratics like Plato and Aristotle. Aristotle believed in knowledge for the sake of knowledge, he was a serious investigator motivated by a consummate desire to discover everything under the sun. Aristotle was a realist with a curiosity about all natural phenomena, and it is inconceivable that he would have accepted the eleventh Principle Doctrine of Epicurus:

> If we were not in any way worried by our suspicions about celestial phenomena and death, fearing lest these things are important for us, and also by our inability to understand that sufferings and desires have a limited character, we should have no need of the study of nature.[4]

Since the Renaissance, Aristotle's influence has diminished, in fact one modern school of philosophy, General Semantics, views him as an enemy to scientific research and theoretical inquiry. For centuries, however, Aristotle enjoyed a greater prestige than any other thinker in history. Not only were his scientific ideas accepted as gospel but he was looked upon as the prototype scientist, the man driving back the veil of ignorance. By comparison, Epicurus was never accepted as a thinker pushing ahead the frontiers of science. He was ridiculed because his aim in scientific investigation was solely to meet a practical end - freedom from fear - and the drive for scientific discovery as an independent challenge never interested him.

EPICURUS AS A PRAGMATIST

Since the aim of all study of the physical environment was to alleviate fear and dismiss the conjecture that supernatural intervention determined the lives of men, Epicurus might be considered a pragmatist. After all, his only reason for scientific investigation was the pragmatic principle of working for a practical end. At first glance it would appear that Epicurus taught with the same view in mind as the famous fifth century B.C. teachers known as Sophists. These men were popularizers of philosophy and they tried to make the subject applicable and meaningful to the masses in the market place. The Sophists are identified as among the first philosophical pragmatists. Before the suggestion is made that Epicurus was a pragmatist (speaking in the same generalization that calls Plato an idealist and Aristotle a realist), one important factor must be studied. Without question, the Garden teacher was a dogmatist and such a stance is incompatible with pragmatic philosophy as defined by the theorists Charles Peirce, William James, and John Dewey.

The theory of "ideas" from Plato, which during Epicurus' time had turned the Academy into a school preaching skepticism; and the "form" and "matter" theory of Aristotle and his Lyceum, were all alien to teachings in the Garden. Clarification of the laws of nature in such a way so that they would contribute to the serenity of mind and subsequent happiness of the student was the aim of Epicurean philosophy. Students were taught the scientific facts, believed the explanations without question, and thus were freed from worry about the unknown. Because Epicureans were required to accept the tenets of science in the letters to Herodotus and Pythocles, never questioning the research methods or results of the experimental inquiry, the school was dogmatic in its teaching. Since dogmatism is antithetical to pragmatism, the Epicurean school members could not be called, as some scholars have insisted, the "Pragmatists of Antiquity." Epicurus was proud of the fact that at a time when other philosophical schools questioned the basis for every positive and assertive statement, his followers accepted the Epicurean dogma without question.

FLEE FROM EVERY FORM OF CULTURE

Epicurus accepted the study of physics, particularly the branch related to the material conditions of the physical universe, and he advocated that all students should study natural phenomena. His reason was the practical wish to rid his students from fear of the gods and supernatural myths; yet, most Greek schools of his time paid little attention to physics and, instead, instructed youth in the subjects of mathematics, music, gymnastics and, on higher education levels, in rhetoric and logic. Music, which included reading and writing (as well as poetry, drama, history, oratory and even some of the sciences), was the most important branch of learning. Along with mathematics, which was the favorite subject of Plato, the music study cultivated the powers of aesthetic appreciation and verbal expression which was the mark of a man of culture. The man of culture had memorized portions from Homer and Hesiod, could recite poetic lyrics as he strummed a lyre, and could argue forcefully with rhetorical skill in logical fashion. This was "Culture" to the Athenian, and he was proud that his sophistication separated him from uneducated Greeks, like the Spartans; or barbarians, like the Persians. Into this climate of opinion Epicurus arrived and established himself as a heretic by commanding his students to avoid culture!

In a fragment of a Letter to Pythocles (not the same letter where he revealed the facts of atmospheric and meteorological conditions), Epicurus told the young student to jump in a boat and sail away from the culture taught by most Athenian schools. The Master was suggesting that Pythocles avoid the sacred aesthetic development which Athenian society felt was so important. The Garden philosopher despised almost all branches of traditional education, and in one letter to Apelles Epicurus praises the young man because he has stayed away from those studies which "contaminate" the Epicureans. Evidently, Apelles had not received a traditional education in the mathematic and music schools, because the Master complimented the student on his avoidance of what the Garden believed was the pernicious influence of the Athenian cultural curricula.

Cicero ridiculed Epicurus' opposition to the traditional curricula; the Stoic was particularly incensed that the leader of the Garden taught no logic. Cicero, as a Roman orator and persuasive writer, could not understand why a teacher would dismiss the importance of the standard rules of logical inquiry, such as deduction and syllogistic inference. It was difficult for the Master's contemporaries to understand his objections to traditional education. In particular, they could not reason why Metrodorus, Epicurus' closest friend and follower, would make the statement that he had never read a line of Homer and did not know whether Hector was a Trojan or a Greek. Such a suggestion was blasphemy because the Iliad and the Odyssey were the central educational works and shaped the ideals for Athenian society. Epicurus did not completely avoid the Homeric epics, rather he extracted certain passages which lent credence to

24

his philosophy, however, on the whole; music, poetry, mathematics, rhetoric, logic, as well as most technical knowledge was unimportant for Epicurean study.

DIOGENES THE CYNIC, OPPONENT TO CULTURE

Only one other ancient Greek philosopher-teacher despised the traditional cultural subject matter in the schools of Hellas. This was Diogenes of Sinope, the Cynic of Athens and Corinth, who railed against the mores and folkways of Greek life. Diogenes the Cynic taught the sons of Xeniades to ride, shoot with the bow, and hurl the javelin because those were practical skills needed in developing strength of body and eye. His schoolroom, however, did not provide for the study of music, geometry, astronomy, and the popular curricula, because Diogenes said the subjects were useless and unnecessary. The only necessary subject, according to the Cynic philosopher, was developmental independence from unrestrained human desires. By demanding that his students be content with plain food, and water to drink; to walk barefoot even in cold weather; to wear the lightest and least adorned clothing, Diogenes of Sinope cultivated an appreciation and enjoyment of the simple, carefree life. He taught that happiness can be found in avoiding material possessions and ignoring the traditional values of hunger for power, status, and wealth.

Diogenes the Cynic, like Epicurus, avoided traditional educational patterns in his philosophy; actually both condemned all teaching of the literature, music, mathematics, and science subjects popular in the schools of their day. Both philosophers shared the conviction that more human unhappiness would result from pursuing popular studies than from an avoidance of those subjects. In other words, happiness is such an important criteria that if the curricula cannot contribute to improved human happiness, the school instructional program should be changed or eliminated. This conviction of the leader of the Garden School (The relationship between happiness and learning) was central to the understanding of his philosophy.

25

EUDAEMONIA VIA ATARAXIA

It has been stated that Epicurus the dogmatist "fled from every form of traditional culture." He advocated a pursuit of happiness on his own terms, and as a hedonist, a seeker of pleasure, the Master built his life style around an axiological formula which was meant to provide total joy in living to his students. The formula can be summarized in three words, **eudaemonia via ataraxia**.

Eudaemonia means happiness, and speculation on the subject was a favorite activity of philosophers for thousands of years. Aristotle, in one of his most important books <u>Nicomachean Ethics</u>, discusses happiness in the first chapter; he defines the subject as an active life governed by the use of reason. With proselytizing zeal he outlines the course of human conduct which produces a pleasant state of mind, **eudaemonia**, through the habitual production of good deeds. Aristotle, and all other ancient philosophers, wrestled with the concept of **eudaemonia** but none were able to delimit its features and define it as succinctly as Epicurus. In the <u>Letter to Menoeceus</u>, his epistle of ethics, the leader of the Garden spoke dogmatically about how "health of body and peace of mind" contributed to producing the happy life.

A healthy body was an obvious choice for a condition of happiness and needs little explanation, however the term **ataraxia**, meaning peace of mind, is a different matter. In the concept of **ataraxia** Epicurus' total system of axiology was developed. Epicurean philosophy can be summarized by the term, **eudaemonia via ataraxia**, that is, happiness is found by way of peace of mind. The letters to Herodotus and Pythocles have been previously described as statements of natural science principle giving students insight into the causes for frightening physical occurrences, such as earthquake, lightning, and eclipses. When Epicurus said that the study of physics and phenomena of the sky was necessary to develop peace of mind and confidence, as well as when he said that the pursuit of scientific investigation was a means to live free from trouble, his reference was to **ataraxia**. In the letters,

in the Principal Doctrines, and in all fragments
from his writings the concept of ataraxia is mentioned
over and over again.

ORIGIN OF ATARAXIA

Many ancient philosophers used the idea of
ataraxia in their philosophy of axiological conduct.
Two philosophers who influenced Epicurus - Democritus
and Pyrrho - used the concept as the very basis
for their philosophical systems.

Democritus was born in Thrace around 460 B.C.
With his teacher Leucippus, Democritus is credited
with popularizing the atomic theory, however, it
is in his theory of ethics that Democritus proposed
the idea which was to influence Epicurus' philosophy
of ataraxia to such a significant degree. From
the fragments which remain from the writings of
Democritus are a number of quotations dealing with
euthumia, a Greek word difficult to translate because
it implies several meanings. Diogenes Laertius
suggests the term refers to the state where one
is calm and undisturbed by fear or other emotions;
while Cicero calls euthumia freedom from alarm.
Also implied, however, is joy and good humor,
therefore, the word is sometimes translated as
cheerfulness.

Because of his philosophy of euthumia
(cheerfulness), Democritus has been called the
laughing philosopher. Seneca in his Moral Essays
compares Heraclitus (the weeping philosopher) with
the laughing philosopher, Democritus. Heraclitus
could not bear the sight of wretched lives and
miserable conditions under which he saw many men
living. For this reason, out of pity, he would
weep in public; while Democritus, on the other hand,
always laughed in public because men lived such
silly, vacuous lives that he did not think there
was any reason for seriousness.

Euthumia, suggested Democritus, allows man
the opportunity to be content and unruffled in the
face of misfortune. It provides "imperturbable
wisdom" to face life's adversities and suffer as
little as possible from the disturbances which
threaten the equanimity of other men. Democritus

27

assured his readers that if they kept their minds in a placid, tranquil state of good cheer, unmoved by desire (that which is not readily attainable) and fear (the threat of body or mental harm), life can be happily rich and rewarding.

Doubtless, this theme struck a convincing note with Epicurus, because his Letter to Menoeceus follows the same line of reasoning, with **ataraxia** representing the same soul-saving axiological position as **euthumia** represented in the writings of Democritus. Both words are very similar in definition and offer the same key to happiness - tranquillity of mind and unruffled human nature.

Epicurus began his study of philosophy by reading the works of Democritus; in addition, he turned eagerly to the teachings of Pyrrho. Nausiphanes, one of Epicurus' early teachers, reported that as a student the future philosopher of the Garden continually asked him for information about Pyrrho. Pyrrho was one of the founders of the Skeptic School, and although Epicureans would not follow the tenets of his philosophy (which preached no dogma - except refusal to accept dogma), they could admire the character and life style of the leader of the school. Many stories were told about the composure and tranquillity of the Skeptic. For instance, once on board a ship during a very bad storm all the passengers were in fear for their lives, except for the placid and serene Pyrrho who pointed to a small pig and told his fellow travelers they should live in an unperturbed state like the animal.

Pyrrho spent a great deal of time discussing **ataraxia**, which was a central feature to his Skepticism. What the Skeptic taught was the disavowal of all philosophical speculation, because none of it, according to him, is necessary in the conduct of everyday life, indeed, metaphysical inquiry hinders the opportunity to arrive at **eudaemonia** or **ataraxia**. This idea, along with Pyrrho's notion that all sense perception was completely unreliable as a source of epistemological truth, was quite the opposite from Epicurus' teaching. In fact, the only common ground between Epicurus and Pyrrho was the same goal in life - **ataraxia** - and both took completely different roads to reach that goal. Pyrrho suspended judgment on all sensory experience, suggesting that by not passing judgment on any event **ataraxia** would follow the course of his life like a shadow.

Epicurus, with the opposite point of view, remarked that only through understanding and believing in the essential elements of nature could one expect to find **ataraxia**.

ATARAXIA IN THE FAR EAST

There is nothing in the philosophy of Democritus, except for **ataraxia**, which is found in the Skepticism of Pyrrho. However, both found their way to tranquillity from the same source. The historian of ancient Greek philosophers, Diogenes Laertius, mentions that both visited the Far East in what is now the country of India. Pyrrho went on his visit with Anaxarchus, who, ironically, might have been a former pupil of Democritus. Perhaps Pyrrho, who was very young when Democritus died, was inspired to take the trip East when he heard about the older philosopher's experience many years before. Whatever the case, both men visited the "Gymnosophists" (naked teachers) in India and very likely the principle of **ataraxia** was derived from this source.

Tranquillity, serenity, and detachment are, of course, important features in the Buddhist philosophy-religion. Regardless of the Buddhist school - Zen, Theravada, Mahayana, Vajrayana - one finds aphorisms and stories extolling the idea of the human mind in perfect composure and placidity. In addition to Buddhism, the entire color of Indian philosophy reflects the concept of **ataraxia** as a pattern of life. In The Mind of India, author William Gerber lists the significant currents of Indian philosophy and in his thesis number "Five" mentions the way to eliminate attachment. The author states, "In the west, this corresponds to the philosophy of contentment. Stoicism (here the author should have mentioned Skepticism and Epicureanism, as well) teaches contentment by advocating **ataraxia**, non-attachment."[5]

EPICUREAN ATARAXIA AS PLEASURE

Epicurus' ethics, like the Master's scientific theory, were written in a clear, positive style giving no student cause for difficulty in

29

interpretation. Happiness (**eudaemonia**), he believed, is found through peace of mind or cheerful contentment (**ataraxia**); the disturbed, fearful or troubled mind cannot achieve either goal. Therefore, according to the theory, every activity should provide an opportunity for **ataraxia** while avoiding the opposite condition. The implication is that one must avoid fearful and troubling conditions, like physical pain, and at the same time pursue activities which will result in peace of mind. Avoiding pain and fear is a form of quietism, an idea often expressed in Eastern philosophy and religion. In the Letter to Menoeceus, after stating that the way to find happiness is by health of body and peace of mind, Epicurus suggests this condition can be met by avoiding the opposite conditions and living in a state of quietism.

> It is to gain this end, namely freedom from pain and fear, that we act as we do. When once this condition is reached the tempest in the soul is quieted since the living creature has no need to go in search of something that is lacking, nor to look for anything else by which he may supplement the good of the soul and the good of the body.[6]

Although it would be difficult for a non-Epicurean to envision, the above quotation is Epicurus' definition of pleasure; that is: freedom from pain in the body and anxiety in the mind. Two more quotations from the Letter to Menoeceus give a clearer indication of how the philosopher states his pleasure principle in terms of negative rather than positive sensations.

> Pleasure is the beginning and the end of the happy life. . . . When we maintain that pleasure is the end, we do not mean the pleasure of the profligate or the pleasures of sensuality, as we are understood to do by some who are either ignorant of our doctrine, or who are not in agreement with it, or willfully misinterpret it. We mean, on the other hand, pleasure consisting of freedom from pain in the body and from anxiety in the mind.[7]

> The pleasant life is not produced by continual drinking and dancing, nor sexual intercourse, nor rare dishes of sea food and other delicacies of a luxurious table. On the contrary, it is produced by sober reasoning which examines the motives

for every choice and avoidance, driving away beliefs
which are the source of mental disturbances.[8]

At the heart of Epicurean philosophy is the idea
of seeking pleasure to find happiness. For his
use of the word "pleasure" the Master has been
castigated by generations of spokesmen for religious
and philosophical societies who interpreted his
pleasure to mean active, dynamic, physical pleasure.
It is obvious that Epicurus meant quite the opposite
by pleasure; he defined the word to mean quiet,
static avoidance of physical sensations. Pleasure
is found not in the body, except for avoidance of
pain, rather, it is found in the mind. Therefore,
pleasure is mental contentment or **ataraxia**. Since
pleasure is the avoidance of painful and troubling
physical and mental disability, happiness is a
negative quality called **ataraxia**. Seneca voices
exactly the same theme as Epicurus when he states,
"The pleasures of the wise man are calm, moderate,
almost listless and subdued, and scarcely noticeable
inasmuch as they come unsummoned. . . ."[9]

PLEASURE VERSUS PAIN

Ataraxia, advised the Master, does not have
to be sought, as in the case of treasure; the
fortunate condition supplying happiness is available
without any more effort than avoiding pain and fear.
This, however, must be qualified with the Epicurean
admonition that pain sometimes leads to peace of
mind and health of body in the future.

> Every pleasure is good because it has a natural
> kinship to us, but not every pleasure is to be chosen;
> in the same way every pain is an evil, yet not all
> pain is to be avoided.[10]

> For this reason there are times when we do not
> choose every pleasure, but avoid those which
> lead to unnecessary discomfort in the long
> run. Furthermore, we consider certain states
> of pain to be preferable to pleasure when greater
> satisfaction results as a consequence of the
> submission to pain.[11]

There are obvious examples to cite for the
reason pain is sometimes necessary as an immediate

31

need which can result in increased happiness in the future. In fact, the practices of the medical profession are predicated upon the assumption that it is better to face limited surgical pain in the present than suffer serious pain in the future from an untreated ailment. Epicurus was a man who knew how to live with pain because his body was delicate and weak from his earliest years. It is not surprising that he gave so much attention to the nature of physical discomfort and, although the absence of pain was his criteria for pleasure, he was able to live with his infirmities with a cheerful heart.

There is an important distinction between living in happiness with pain, as opposed to finding pain pleasurable. Epicurus once said that even in the torture chamber a man can be happy although he may cry in pain. Cicero and Seneca, the Roman Stoics, later ridiculed those remarks by maintaining that it is impossible for a man under torture to find any enjoyment in his pain. Seneca mentions that he would rather have joy than pain, but if torture is a consequence of virtuous action, one must face it with Stoic forbearance and live with the necessary misery. Epicurus, on the other hand, said a man could cry and groan (an animated display of weakness which the proud Stoics would never allow), yet, the tortured man could be happy with the memory of his friends and the good life he has lead. The Master recognized the pain of torture, which obviously forbad pleasure, yet he also insisted that happiness could still be found existent when pleasure was absent. Cicero and Seneca looked upon pleasure and happiness as the same sensation, while Epicurus recognized that there is a significant difference between them. In addition, the leader of the Garden suggested there is no reason to fear or find unhappiness in pain, because severe pain causes an early death which frees one from suffering and long-enduring pain is usually tolerable to the brave. To clarify his position, the Master wrote as his fourth Principal Doctrine the admonition:

> Pain does not prevail continuously in the flesh
> but the peak of it is present for the briefest
> interval, and the pain that barely exceeds the
> pleasure in the flesh is not with us many days,
> while protracted illnesses have an excess of
> pleasure over pain in the flesh.[12]

ATARAXIA THROUGH LIMITING DESIRE

It has been mentioned that the tranquil spirit, so important to the happiness of an Epicurean, is not something that must be looked for and sought with effort. On the contrary, one simply avoids pain, except under the necessary condition of accepting present pain to insure future pleasure, and very little extra effort to find happiness is necessary. The relentless pursuit of happiness by conscious effort and vigorous endeavor is absolutely unnecessary, according to the Garden philosopher. Nothing could be more alien to his ideas than a striving to find pleasure in worldly desires. Epicurus names three different levels of desires: those which are natural and necessary, those which are natural but unnecessary, and those which are unnatural and unnecessary.

The desires which are natural and necessary refer to the basic needs for the preservation of life: food, clothing, and shelter; plus the health of body (freedom from pain) and tranquillity of mind. Other desires which are natural; such as sexual pleasure, enjoyment of rich food and drink, and amusements for idle hours are not in themselves evil, but they are unnecessary. The third level of desires, however, can be harmful. These include the desires which would be called unnatural and unnecessary; such as: greed for money, status, power, and fame. The Greek teacher insisted that natural but unnecessary, and (especially) the unnatural and unnecessary desires, offer intense immediate pleasure, but they are short-lived and can, in the long run, inhibit **ataraxia**. Doubtless, stories were related in the Garden School with reference to showing that indulgence in rich food and drink bring intense immediate pleasure, but several hours later the pain from gluttony or drunkenness will cancel previous enjoyment. It is also unquestioned that the Master admonished against pursuit of wealth and public recognition, arguing that such unnecessary pleasures are ephemeral and often lead to mental stress and pain.

To aid in showing the danger of unrestrained

desire, Epicurus offered numerous maxims (some of which were rather platitudinous) which fit consistently into his philosophy of limiting desire to insure **ataraxia**. The following are particularly relevant to the dangerous third category of desires, those which are unnatural and unnecessary.

> The acquisition of riches for many men has not been an escape from their troubles, but only a change to greater troubles.[13]

> If you wish to make Pythocles rich, do not give him more money, but take away from his desires.[14]

> The vexation of the soul cannot be resolved, nor any true joy produced by the possession of the greatest wealth, or by honor and esteem in the eyes of the public, or by any of the things connected with unrestrained desire.[15]

When Ecclesiastes 6:9 suggests, "It is better to be satisfied with what is before your eyes than give rein to desire," it is the same condemnation of pursuing vain and unnatural desires which Epicurus speaks about in the foregoing quotations, and, in similar fashion, in a preserved fragment from a letter when he advises that the man who is not satisfied with a little - is never satisfied.

From the preceding comments it would appear obvious that happiness for Epicurus was not difficult to achieve. Even with his bodily ailments, the ecstatic joy of mental pleasure, **ataraxia**, kept him in cheerful spirits as he went about recommending to his students to "live with a smile." To the man desperately seeking happiness, the philosopher advised restraint and quiet contemplation of the present life circumstance. Epicurus felt that the few basic human needs could be met with little effort, and controlling the imagination of man, which was usually consumed with unfulfilled desires, would bring peace of mind. The alternative, according to the Master, was a life of aimless hunger for imaginings, stretching on forever.

Around him, Epicurus could see the machinations of an active, stressful, competitive society; intrigue and political conniving were commonplace. Athens was a city-state where ambitious politicians, greedy commercial businessmen, and opportunistic military leaders vied for success. People sought pleasure in games, amusements, and a relaxed standard of sexual morality. Menander, Epicurus' friend from military school, wrote plays in which Athenian society was pictured as a life of wine, women, and song. It was plain that the mass of men wanted happiness but sought pleasure in false gods. Epicurus was ready with an alternative life style, in fact, he listed it as the twenty-first rule of his <u>Principle Doctrines</u>: "One who understands the limits of life knows how easy it is to obtain that which removes the pain arising from want and to make the whole of life perfect. Therefore, there is no need of competing for success."[16] While Athenian life bustled around him; while the dictator of Athens, Demetrius Poliorcetes, taxed the citizens hundreds of thousands of dollars on the grounds that his mistress needed the money for soap, Epicurus advised withdrawal from the competitive struggles, and quiet living devoted to cultivating peace of mind.

ATARAXIA IN THE GARDEN OF LEISURE

In the Garden students pursued the course of spiritual and mental perfection. Since Epicurus had outlawed myths, superstitions, and religious rituals the spiritual perfection sought by all students was conformity to the tenets of the Master with his emphasis on finding peace of mind. The school was a training ground in learning restraint and seeking the truth which freed the mind from fear and worry. Disciples pursued their studies; learning to separate fact from fiction about the physical nature of the world, learning to free the mind from fears and troubles, and learning to live according to the tenets of the Master. Always the aim was the same - to find happiness (**eudaemonia**) through the static pleasure of mental quietude (**ataraxia**).

Educational studies at the Garden must have been conducted with a relaxed, non-competitive, leisurely pace. Coercion, threat, or intimidation was antithetical to Epicurean philosophy which believed man has free will and must determine the conduct of his own life without supernatural intervention. Students listened, talked, and discussed in an arena of free inquiry at a leisurely pace. In other words, Epicurus' Garden was an educational example of **schole - sigma, chi, omicron,**

35

lambda, eta. The Greek word **schole** (skole) means free time, discussion, or leisure. As is well-known, this Greek word provided the English word for school. What better word is possible to describe Epicurean education? From the evidence of all writers, the Garden was a "true" school in conformity with the Greek ideals of what **schole** implied. The pursuit of peace of mind in leisure, **ataraxia** in **schole**, is an apt description of the Garden.

The Garden was not a sweatshop of intellectual effort, where cowering students conned their notes in preparation for examinations by autocratic teachers. On the contrary, students cultivated serenity of spirit in an atmosphere of leisure; under the tutelage of communal friends. Spiritual perfection was the aim, with the life-style of Epicurus held as the ideal for all followers to emulate. The Master of the Garden exemplified the cheerful life of contented contemplation which was the theme of **schole**.

THE SEARCH FOR OBSCURITY

Epicurus believed that man cannot serve two masters, himself and society. Since it was impossible to live for the best interests of the political state without sacrificing individual freedom, the Greek teacher physically and mentally removed himself from the active affairs of the Athenian city-state. It is apparent that Epicurus mandated his followers to avoid most of the business, political, social, and religious activities of Athenian life, because several preserved fragments from his writings attest to the abhorrence he felt toward the life of the city.

Live in Anonymity.[17]

The purest source of attaining security from men, which at times must be established by banishing life's disturbing elements, is secured by the quiet life and withdrawal from the mob.[18]

We must free ourselves from the prison of business affairs and politics.[19]

We must state the best way a man will reach the aim of a good life, and how no person would want to hold public office.[20]

The first quotation is a famous Epicurean motto first quoted by Plutarch. In Greek the expression is "lathe biosas," which is translated: live unknown, live unnoticed, live in obscurity, or live in anonymity. The other related fragments support the Epicurean position that the scramble for public acclaim; the quest for riches and power, threaten the security of an individual and attack his peace of mind. Here, once again, is an example of how **ataraxia** determined the attitude and course of action for followers of the Master. Instead of serving the city of Athens in an active role, the Epicureans turned their backs on the life of the metropolis to live in quiet serenity in the Garden. In fact, life was so quiet that Epicurus lived in accordance with his axiom, "lathe biosas," by remaining virtually unknown during his thirty-five years in the city. Seneca reports:

> This man (Epicurus), however, was unknown to
> Athens itself, near which he had hidden himself
> away. And so, when he had already survived
> many years his friend Metrodorus, he added in
> a letter these last words, proclaiming with
> thankful appreciation the friendship that had
> existed between them: 'So greatly blest were
> Metrodorus and I that it has been no harm to us
> to be unknown, and almost unheard of, in this
> well-known land of Greece.'[21]

To achieve **ataraxia** Epicurus risked censure for his retreat from active social service to the city-state. The philosopher believed that only in a congenial community of friends, living abstemiously, and devoting time to reflection and philosophical discussion could a student develop spiritual perfection; that is, **eudaemonia via ataraxia**. The temptations and allure of the busy city could only harm the student in his quest for contentment and truth.

The Epicurean attitude was plain living and high thinking in a rural communal community. A parallel may be suggested here, for the Garden was similar to a famous nineteenth century American experiment in living. "Plain living and high thinking" was the slogan (adopted from William Wordsworth) used by Brook Farm, an experiment in transcendentalist philosophical living in West

37

Roxbury, Massachusetts in the 1840's. Like the Garden of Epicurus, Brook Farm was an experimental community of men and women, growing their own food, striving for spiritual perfection within the tenets of philosophy rather than religion, and operating an excellent preparatory school. One important difference between the two "communes" was the difference in educational aim. The Garden of Epicurus attempted to educate the individual for personal freedom of mind and tranquillity of spirit by ignoring the traditional learning, while Brook Farm's main purpose was preserving the classical cultural values.

An American transcendentalist who knew the members of Brook Farm, but who decided not to join the commune, was a solitary and poetic thinker who shared many of Epicurus' ideas. This was Henry David Thoreau, who spent much of his life, including two years living in a cabin at Walden Pond in Massachusetts, writing and reflecting on the human condition. One opinion which Thoreau shared with Epicurus was the conviction that, "The mass of men lead lives of quiet desperation."[22] In several excerpts from letters, Epicurus voices his disdain for the empty lives most men lead:

> Everywhere you can find men who live for empty desires and have no interest in the good life. Stupid fools are those who are never satisfied with what they possess, but only lament what they cannot have.[23]

> I never wished to please the mob, for what I know, they do not approve, and what they approve, I do not know (how to perform).[24]

> When you find yourself among the mob, this is the best time for withdrawing into yourself.[25]

Both Thoreau and Epicurus distrusted the "mob" and both wished to live within the prescription of **lathe biosas**. Thoreau said, "Public opinion is a weak tyrant compared with our own private opinion. What a man thinks of himself, that it is which determines, or rather indicates, his fate."[26]

When a man chooses to ignore the standard behavioral patterns of society; when he views much of the conduct of worldly affairs with contempt, he often imagines himself as fighting a lonely battle against the corruption and vice of the outside world.

Such an independence of spirit, with such iconoclastic impulses, has produced rebels with cynical and jaded views of society. Many outspoken critics who condemn the vain pursuits of their fellow men become "weeping philosophers," like Heraclitus, with pessimistic, unhappy attitudes about the purpose of life. This is certainly not a characteristic of Epicurean philosophy. The Master always maintained his cheerfulness (**euthumia**) and, although still doubtful whether his fellow men applied their lives to the most philosophically satisfying pursuits, Epicurus spoke with optimistic positivism when he said, "We must laugh and at the same time philosophize, managing our households and carrying out our other duties, while never ceasing to expound the words of the true philosophy."[27]

The words of his "true philosophy" advocated **lathe biosas**, because only by keeping out of the public eye did the individual protect himself from the misfortunes and adversity of corruption and vice. While most men groveled for vain desires, Epicurus and his followers physically and mentally removed themselves from the arena of civic action. The students of the Garden were not adventurous, gallant, brave explorers looking for public acclaim through valiant deeds, as exemplified in the <u>Iliad</u> and <u>Odyssey</u>. Not only did the activity of the marketplace or battle field offer no attraction, the physical competition of sports was ignored. Although Epicurus believed in the importance of a healthy body, and moderate exercise would certainly have been encouraged at the school, the purpose of sports, according to the philosophy of the Garden, should be to provide **bona mens**, **bona valetudo** (a healthy mind and a healthy body) and not a physically competitive spectacle. A number of inscriptions extolling the creed **bona mens**, **bona valetudo** have been excavated in Epicurean settlements from ancient Rome.

Since training the mind to be serene and content with the fortunes of nature - removed from the hurry-scurry life of the city - was the aim of the Garden, many commentators have ridiculed the philosophy as dull and unexciting. However, Epicurus' attitude toward adventure and excitement was not a condemnation of all public entertainment and amusements which most people enjoy. In fact, the Master, according to Diogenes Laertius, enjoyed public ceremonies and there is reason to believe he joined in religious observances; even to the point of attending the Dionysiac festivals. Therefore, Epicurus was not opposed to the excitement of public spectacles, he recognized that happiness can result from observation and participation in some public events. However, the mental attitude of the Epicurean observer would be different from the mass of men, because the followers of the Master would quietly and contentedly watch (maybe participate), but never lose their **ataraxia** and anonymity.

The leader of the Garden was not a recluse, living a hermitical life behind the walls of his school. In his three-wheeled chair he was, likely, a familiar sight on Athenian streets. However, the principle of **lathe biosas** prevailed as the criteria of his conduct, and he lived and traveled in obscurity without involvement in the turbulent politics and social life of his day. At one time Epicurus even suggested that a wise man will not speak in public, unless requested to do so; and then not in such a way as to proselytize.

Since most Epicureans avoided public service and attempted to live in obscurity (that is, if they wished to follow the Master's teaching), many of their philosophical opponents accused students of the Garden with shirking civic responsibility. Especially during Roman times, led by the bitter denunciations of Plutarch and Epictetus, Epicureans were condemned as traitors to the idea of participatory government. Epictetus with righteous indignation proclaimed:

> In the name of Zeus, I ask you, can you imagine
> an Epicurean State?. . . .The doctrines are bad,
> subversive of the State, destructive to the family,
> not even fit for women. Drop these doctrines,
> man. You live in an imperial State; it is your duty
> to hold office, to judge uprightly. . . .[28]

Stoics, like Epictetus, continually referred to "duty" and "service" in public life, which they viewed as the highest good - which means working for the improvement of the human condition in civil service.

However, the most inflammatory criticism of the Master was given by the famous Roman writer and educator, Plutarch. In Plutarch's <u>Moralia</u> several essays focus on alleged calumnies of the Epicurean school and in one treatise, "That Epicurus Actually Makes a Pleasant Life Impossible," the author suggests that the doctrine of the Garden is little less than a crime against humanity! Critics, like Epictetus and Plutarch, were incensed by what they interpreted as an egoistic theme in the Master's philosophy, when, to their beliefs, altruism was the most valued sentiment in ethics. The Roman writers railed against what they saw as the selfish factor in Garden school ethics.

The altruist voices his belief in personal sacrifice for the benefit of others, accusing the egoist of solely selfish motives in human relations. However, many altruistic arguments are simplistic, because many of the actions by people using altruism as a rationale have been anything but beneficial to general human happiness. Many wars, and some of history's destructive ventures into supposedly improving the condition of life, have been perpetuated by men working from what they claimed were solely altruistic motives. The lesson is obvious - because mankind is very different in many cultural features the same code of charitable effort in one social context will produce results which may not be noble, elevated, and admirable in another cultural setting. The opposite is also true; the egoist, who works from personal motives, does not necessarily beat his wife, abuse his friends, and steal from public coffers because he believes in pursuing his own interests. The virtues of Epicurean egoism appear equally charitable to the altruism of their rivals - the Stoics.

A FRIEND MUST DIE FOR A FRIEND

As an egoist who distrusted the affairs of the masses; lived in anonymity as a protection against pervasive societal influences which would undermine his ethics, Epicurus refused to attempt altruistic public endeavors. He was not against others performing public service, but he felt, like Thoreau, that, "As for Doing-good. . . .it does not agree with my constitution."[29] The idea of social service was the **summum bonum** for Roman Stoics; but it was not for the Master and his students. This is not to say, however, that the Epicureans followed an

41

egoistic direction in ethical conduct in the normal understanding of the concept. Quite the contrary, egoism in the Garden was pursuit of **eudaemonia via ataraxia**, but without the selfish individualism with which egoism is associated in modern psychological and philosophical thought. The pleasure principle of Epicurus finds expression not in isolation of the individual seeking mental serenity, but, rather, in shared experiences of the tranquil life. Disciples of the Garden believed happiness was achieved in their own obscure social context; **lathe biosas** was not isolation from all men, but only from those men in the mad, corrupt world where unnatural and unnecessary desires predominated.

The society of the Garden was a quiet, retiring community of shared **ataraxy**; it was friendship among like-minded colleagues, living together and working toward a common goal of peace of mind. Friendship is absolutely essential for complete satisfaction in living, according to the writings of Epicurus. It is in the concept of friendship that the claim of Epicurean egoism, as an enemy to human welfare, finds refutation. Because of his views on friendship the Master must be placed among those charitable few people willing to sacrifice the most precious of possessions, one's own life, for the happiness of others. Three quotations, garnered from different sources, picture the unusual qualities of generosity exhibited by the Greek teacher.

> One must on occasion be willing to die for a friend.[30]

> . . .Epicurus, who places happiness in the deepest quiet, as in a sheltered and landlocked harbour, says that it is not only nobler, but also pleasanter, to confer than to receive benefits.[31]

> The wise man is not more pained when being tortured (himself, than when seeing) his friend (tortured): (but if his friend does him wrong), his whole life will be confounded by distrust and completely upset.[32]

The first quotation, from Diogenes Laertius' Lives, appears as a direct contradiction to the theme of egoism; after all, if one gives up his life for another the gesture appears altruistic rather than egoistic. However, as is true in the Vatican Collection fragment in the third quotation the wise man is willing to make his sacrifices for a "friend." Epicurus (as the second quotation, from Plutarch, declares) believed that "it is better to give than to receive," yet he would have remained true to his egoistic hedonism by making the choice of how, when, and to whom he would "confer benefits" and sacrifice his life. Doubtless his choice would have been limited to friends. Therefore as a humanitarian, Epicurus was a model of self-sacrifice and altruism when he could name the conditions.

FRIENDSHIP NECESSARY FOR HAPPINESS

The condition and criteria for all human conduct at the Garden was **philia**, loving friendship. Epicurus began by admitting that, "Every friendship is desirable for itself, but it starts from personal need."[33] In other words, friendships are first made to help the individual gain a direct benefit from the association. By this suggestion the philosopher meant that mutual aid and assistance is necessary to supply the basic needs of life. He recognized that friends offer support and assistance in times when even the most self-sufficient individual cannot control the circumstances of his existence. Security, safety, and peace of mind to pursue perfection of the soul would be impossible without a cooperative endeavor. For this reason, Epicurus suggested as his last Principal Doctrine, number forty, the following:

> All those who have the ability to find security from people who live near them, possess a most agreeable life together, since they enjoy natural friendship; and if one of their company should die early, the survivors will not lament the demise as some heartbreaking occurrence.[34]

The Master, who cherished rich personal friendships with many people in many lands, must have been thinking about Metrodorus, his closest friend and disciple who died seven years before Epicurus, when he wrote the above words.

From an original impulse to further personal security with friendship, the Epicurean doctrine taught that the next stage was the benefit of individual happiness derived from the collective

43

well-being of friends. Another Principal Doctrine, number twenty-seven, states, "Of everything that wisdom offers to produce for a life of happiness, the greatest is the possession of friendship."[35] From the first cautious acceptance of friendship as an aid in facing a threatening world, to the happiness found in **philia**; the Epicurean school, unlike any other institution in antiquity, made friendship an absolutely necessary ingredient to the pleasures of mind and body. Seneca quotes Epicurus as saying:

> You must reflect carefully beforehand with whom
> you are to eat and drink, rather than what you are
> to eat and drink. For a dinner of meats without
> the company of a friend is like the life of a lion
> or a wolf.[36]

It seems odd that Epicurus would refer to eating meat when he has been credited with subsisting on a diet of barley meal, water, and an occasional piece of cheese, but his resolute point of sharing pleasure with a friend is quite definitive. As well as sharing all fortunes with a friend, Epicurus, according to Diogenes Laertius, advised that one should never give up a friend and together the partnership can lead to a mutual enjoyment of life's pleasures.

Book VIII and Book IX of Nicomachean Ethics by Aristotle deal with friendship, including the idea that ultimately friendly relations are based on self-love. Aristotle explores the different kinds of friendship and exalts the relationship as an important factor in human happiness. But, unquestionably, it was the leader of the Garden who showed the greatest rapture and exhibited the highest praise for **philia**. The following are a number of the expressions in tribute to friendship which remain among the extant fragments of Epicurus' writings:

> Too much haste and too much slowness in forming
> a friendship are equally blameworthy; we must be
> ready even to run risks to preserve friendship.[37]

> Friendship joyously dances around the world
> proclaiming to everyone that they should awake
> to recognize the joys of a happy life.[38]

Wisdom and friendship are the chief concerns of
the good man; of these one is a mortal good, and
the other represents an immortal good.[39]

FRIENDS IN THE GARDEN

In essence, the Epicurean fellowship looked
upon friendship as the technique by which
resident-members of the school could grow in
philosophical maturity. Recognizing that only the
exceptional man, like Epicurus, can arrive at
realization of the truth on his own, the membership
strove together to find the true path. Education,
therefore, was a cooperative venture. By sharing
social, emotional, and intellectual experiences
the students grew in their understanding of the
cult dogma, as well as in perfecting their own
self-realization. Friendship was more than an
instrument to propitiate learning - it became an
end in itself. The relationship shared by members
of the school proved their fidelity to one another
and their total commitment to the Epicurean way
of life.

Ironically for a school which accepted a
materialistic, atomistic view of nature; refusing
to accept the mythological, supernatural, or religious
interpretations of natural phenomena; Epicurus and
his followers lived in a brotherhood reminiscent
of medieval monasticism. The Garden was not an
institution filled with the chants and liturgy of
a religious society, but the members did break bread
in a philosophical sacrament of spirituality. If
the friendship and sharing of a mutual life style
among the residents (and visitors) to the Garden
was similar to a monastery during a later Christian
era, there were significant differences as well.
The Epicureans exhibited one departure from custom
which for much of Western history would rarely be
found among fraternal and religious societies living
in a communalistic state - women and slaves were
admitted to the Garden and treated as friends and
equals in pursuit of truth. As mentioned previously,
such an action was almost unheard of among the Greeks
who held the view that the place for woman was in
the home, and the place for a slave was in the
marketplace or house of his owner.

45

Sexual expression during the time of Epicurus in Athens was very free and uninhibited, with homosexual romantic attachment common; particularly between an older man and a boy of school age. This relationship, known as **paederastia**, was not usually condemned as a vice. There is no question, however, that Epicurus opposed homosexuality, and, in fact, all sexual relationships. Surprisingly, there is good reason to believe that to discourage the temptations of the flesh, women were encouraged to study at the Garden where they were accepted as friends. The words defining "love" in Greek refer to erotic love, the love of mankind, and the love of friends. **Philia**, love of friends or friendship, was unquestionably the variety practiced by the Epicureans. Epicurus once said, "Remove sight, social contact, and sexual intercourse, and the passions which inspire love will end."[40] The erotic passion, to which he made reference, was reduced in the Garden by a family relationship among resident-members - the school became a family with mutual love and devotion exhibited between faculty and students. In this way sexual activity was discouraged because residents looked upon one another as brothers and sisters. Obviously, Epicurus represented the head of the household, he was the father to his associates. The other faculty members nurtured the students in the same way as a mother would show care and attention to her children.

An example of this family relationship was the way in which Epicurus addressed his young charges. In preserved fragments from numerous letters, the Greek teacher wrote to his students using very affectionate greetings. To Pythocles, the Master wrote, "Blest youth. . .I will sit down and wait for your lovely and godlike appearance."[41] To another friend a letter was addressed, "Lord and Savior, my dearest Leontion."[42] The leader of the Garden felt such a love for his friends that he addressed them with expressions characteristic of a father to his children.

CHAPTER III

THE GARDEN SCHOOL

The school of Epicurus did not require that
students pass formal entrance requirements or possess
a specific level of academic competence. Quite the
contrary, the Garden welcomed youth free from the
influence of the traditional Greek preparatory
education. Most Athenian boys, starting at the age
of seven, received musical and literary training
at the **didascaleum** (music school) and physical
education at the **palaestra** (exercising ground). By
age fifteen the fundamentals of formal schooling
had provided the basic education which was further
developed by additional physical training at the
gymnasium, and an introduction to philosophy through
tutoring in the basics of rhetoric, geometry, grammar,
dialectic and more music. After a student served
two years of military duty (starting at age eighteen)
he was ready for higher education.

The learner's previous educational experiences
would have provided no advantage in the Epicurean
school because the criteria for admission was not
previous training, but commitment to devote one's
life to the study of philosophy. Epicurus said,
"No one when young should postpone the study of
philosophy, nor grow weary of the study when he is
old, because it is never too early or too late to
secure health of the soul."[1] A healthy body, mind,
and soul was the aim of Garden schooling and the
Master had his doubts as to whether rhetoric, geometry,
grammar, dialectic, and music served to meet this

47

educational goal. Since **bona mens, bona valetudo** was the **summum bonum** for finding happiness, all past educational experiences which did not contribute to that end were thought to be unnecessary.

Cicero, who was usually very critical of Epicurean philosophy, once defended the Greek philosopher by refuting the comments of a fellow Roman with the following statement.

> You are pleased to think him uneducated. The reason is that he refused to consider any education worth the name that did not help to school us in happiness. . . .No! Epicurus was not uneducated: the real philistines are those who ask us to go on studying till old age the subjects that we ought to be ashamed not to have learnt in boyhood.[2]

The neophyte in the Garden felt no shame at his lack of previous schooling, and it was likely that the young man who received an excellent tutorial education gave no evidence of the fact when he arrived at Epicurus' school. Even Polyaenus, the esteemed mathematician, renounced his field of concentration and, as an associate leader in the Garden, probably spent little time in his mathematical studies.

PRIVATE EDUCATION WITHOUT DISCRIMINATION

Public education was an anathema to the Epicureans. After all, if the private education in Athens did little for a youth but impregnate his mind with the useless facts of the cultural heritage from Ionian society, wouldn't public education catering to the tastes of the mob do even more damage to the impressionable mind of the fledgling learner? One had only to look at the abuses of public education in Sparta, where boys lived in barracks and received military training from an early age, to visualize the problems Epicurus wanted to avoid. In Spartan society the mass of citizenry lost individuality and freedom of choice by living subservient to the interests of the state. In Epicurean theory, with the state subservient to the best interests of the individual, mass conformity and stereotyped societal living patterns were viewed with alarm.

Only in his retired private haven, safe from

institutions catering to the tastes of the mob, did Epicurus feel he could pursue his dream of a community of scholars working in joy to perfect their potential for happiness, while sharing the fruits of their studies with a congenial brotherhood. The purpose of the quiet, private school in the Garden was to free the mind from the pernicious influence of a corrupt and jaded society. Even the studies in the traditional schools of Athens perpetuated the false myths of the past. The Epicureans wanted to free the mind from the dogma of the past, which created the unhappy society they observed outside the walls of the Garden. The cry of the Garden was "No more reliance on Homer and Hesiod!" A new creed and dogma, the free choice of **eudaemonia via ataraxia**, was offered as a substitute for the myths and lore which represented the Greek ideals taught in the traditional mode.

Nothing was traditional about the Garden in comparison with most schools of the time. For instance, anyone with the zeal for learning how to live the life of refined pleasure was welcomed. The brotherhood was open to all sexes, nationalities, and races; the wealthy and poor sat side by side next to "barbarians" such as slaves and non-Greeks. Women, who openly flaunted the fact that they were once prostitutes, assembled and joined men of all ages in the quest for Epicurean happiness.

For nearly all of human history schooling has been a privileged opportunity for a select minority. Only since the middle of the nineteenth century has universal education been promoted in Western countries, and in much of the world today opportunity is limited. 2300 years ago Epicurus recognized that all men have an equal right to develop their potential to the highest level of competence. He viewed the intermingling of all people in the quest for philosophical happiness as a necessary feature of his school. The blending of all sexes, nationalities, and races was one ingredient which added life and spirit to his educational system.

PROGRESS AND SELF-REALIZATION

Diogenes Laertius mentions that friends came from all parts of the world to live and study at the Garden. Included were Epicurus' brothers, his slave Mys, and a host of disparate individuals. Perhaps never before, or since, was a more integrated cast of personages assembled to seek the truth of **ataraxia**. The Garden was not a school where students worked toward an academic degree or certificate, rather, the result of their academic endeavors was the intangible reward of truth. Lucretius best expressed the gratitude which a student would feel as his prize for Epicurean study when he told how hearts were "cleansed" by the Master's words of truth.

Evaluation for achievement of the cleansing derived from "words of truth" was based on the student's own assessment of his progress. Each disciple was free to use his own mind; he had the choice of accepting and living in conformity to the dictates of the cult creed, or he could reject part of the Epicurean system. It is obvious that the Master intended total adherence to his ideas, but later history reveals, particularly in the writings of Roman Stoics, that some students made a piecemeal choice of certain tenets; accepting some and rejecting others. This eclecticism often resulted in people calling themselves Epicureans but behaving in an entirely different fashion. Epicurus referred to himself as a dogmatist and expected friends wishing to receive the reward of **ataraxia** to follow his commandments, however, because he believed in freedom of choice and recognized that not all men would wish to follow the route to happiness he prescribed, the Master also suggested that men follow their own "natural dispositions."

The Epicureans were not an evangelical society, they did not sell their wares on the street. If a person wished to listen and obey, the school was ready to give succor. A student would stay as long as he or she needed guidance in the search for self-discovery, self-realization, integration of personality, or whatever other name is applied to the process of living on a level to bring personal fulfillment and happiness.

How does one know when selfhood has been reached? To Epicurus the answer was easy - one knows when he is able to relate to others and to himself on a level that provides complete peace of mind; when his actions are, "the same awake and even when asleep." The ideal is to live like the gods who enjoy perfect peace and contentment and never let human affairs

50

disturb them. When a human can live in such a way
as to function with **euthumia** in **eudaemonia**, that
person knows he has found **ataraxia** and arrived at
self-realization. In the only preserved record of
Epicurus' own words about the axiological foundations
of his philosophy, the Letter to Menoeceus, the Greek
teacher delivers his doctrine of ethics and finishes
the letter with the following peroration:

> Contemplate these and similar precepts day and
> night, both alone and with a friend, and you will
> never be disturbed while awake or asleep. You
> will live like a god among men, for a man who
> lives in the midst of immortal blessings loses
> all semblance of mortality.[3]

Progress on the path to enlightenment, and consequent
self-realization would be evaluated in the Garden
against the standard represented by men, like Epicurus,
who lived "like gods among men."

Plato, in his Republic, was very definitive
about the curriculum, time of service, and other
features of his educational system. In almost every
area he disagreed with Epicurus. Plato's students
studied the traditional subjects to develop the
technique of pure reason, while Epicurus' students
avoided traditional subjects and developed empirical
powers. The Academy accepted gifted students at
age twenty; then by selective screening at age
twenty-five or thirty cultivated an elite corps of
philosopher-kings who practiced philosophy and
dialectics until graduation at age thirty-five. The
graduates were then required to serve the state in
public office. Epicurus' non-selective students
had absolutely no time limit, no graduation, and
certainly no training in service to the state during
their tenure at the Garden.

REFUTATION OF ALL MYTHS AND SUPERSTITION

In attempting to explain the existence of the
world, the Greeks created a story about how in the
beginning there was a state of Chaos. Out of Chaos
the earth, the sky, and the underworld emerged. After
this was the mating of the earth and sky from which
monsters were born, followed by Cyclops, then Titans,
and finally humans. Every Greek child learned about

the "Golden Age" of Greece when Titans and Olympians roamed the earth creating and discovering every useful product, from fire to the cultivation of the olive. Epicurus as a boy heard the stories and because he had an inquisitive mind asked questions of his teachers. In one instance he asked about Chaos and from what source it originated. When his teacher could not provide a satisfactory answer, the future Master of the Garden turned to philosophy as the source of truth.

During his entire life the Greek teacher from Samos questioned the myths and legends which provided answers to questions about the origin and nature of physical phenomena. As was previously mentioned, Epicurus' mother, Chaerestrate, was evidently a charlatan huckster dispensing magic herbs and telling fortunes. Undoubtedly the experience of his youth, assisting his mother in her chicanery, contributed to his doubts about answers to speculative questions emerging from supernatural sources. This attitude by the Master was of inestimable importance when he founded the Garden, because he insisted that all myths and superstitions were to be ignored.

When most Greeks believed that it was necessary to propitiate the favor of the gods and all supernatural forces by ritual, prayer, sacrifice, and other means, the Epicureans argued that such practices were unnecessary. Instead of vengeful, vindictive gods who intruded in the personal affairs of humans and who could, and would, punish men for slight offenses, the Epicureans believed that the gods took no interest in mundane earthly affairs. The gods lived oblivious to mankind in perpetual happiness produced by their calm and tranquil superiority. In other words, it was the gods who had found **eudaemonia via ataraxia** and for this reason they didn't want to become enmeshed in the troublous world of humanity.

Most gods of legend and myth never existed; instead of fictional creations, mankind should worship the true gods of serene good will, advised Epicurus. The first of the Principal Doctrines states that the true gods never know trouble or cause trouble to anyone, and further revelation is given when Epicurus explains the nature of gods and their immortal and blessed life in the Letter to Menoeceus. In addition, Lucretius begins Book One of his Epicurean poetic treatise with a detailed outline of how mankind

should not fear the wrath of gods who are completely
indifferent to human affairs, as well as why men
should not fear the afterlife. Death offered no
sting for the Epicurean because he accepted the fact
that his soul was not immortal, but died with the
body.

Students in the Garden probably did not have
many nightmares depicting the horrors of Hell,
monsters, magical enchantments, or any other vision
of the dark unknown. Epicurus simply would not allow
any feelings or sensations to originate from fear
and he stated this very clearly over and over again
in his writings. An example is the Letter to Herodotus
where, after developing the theme, the Master advises
his student to trust to the senses and to completely
forget the "unreasoning imagination" which causes
fear.

The school of Epicurus immediately took two
steps in the education process whenever a new recruit
for learning arrived at the Garden. First, the student
was directed to forget whatever false information
he had read in stories about Odysseus, Theseus, Jason,
and the hundreds of others who faced danger from
the caprice of the gods and terror from the threat
of monsters. Because legends from the "Golden Age"
of Greek heroes were a predominate part of every
youth's education the student was, in effect, told
to ignore his past schooling. Second, the young
Epicurean learner was re-educated about the true
nature of celestial and earthly phenomena.

VALUE OF BOOKS AND THE PRINCIPAL DOCTRINES

The method of teaching the true nature of the
heavens and earth was through the presentation of
scientific explanations which Epicurus borrowed from
other philosophers, and created himself, to answer
questions about the mysteries of the universe. Such
a wealth of facts required many books (for purposes
of explanation the writings are called books, although
in ancient Greece they were actually rolls of papyrus).
Epicurus wrote thirty-seven books in a series called
On Nature and hundreds of others on all aspects of
scientific inquiry. Since a neophyte could not be
expected to immediately read all the treatises on
science which were continually pouring forth from

53

the hand of Epicurus and his associates, a number
of abridged handbooks served as initial study guides.

The most famous of the study guides was a handbook
which today is about six pages long and can easily
be read in fifteen minutes. This short treatise
is the famous Kuriai Doxai or forty Principal Doctrines
of Epicurean philosophy. It has also been known
by a number of other names such as: Leading Doctrines,
Authorized Doctrines, Sovran Maxims, and the
Authoritative Doctrines. The Kuriai Doxai are forty
statements which summarize the creed and, in Epicurus'
day, started the Garden student on the path to
Epicurean enlightenment.

The work was evidently very famous in antiquity
because it has been mentioned by many authors. Cicero
insisted that his friend Torquatas should be familiar
with the words, "for every good Epicurean has got
by heart the Master's Kuriai Doxai, since these brief
aphorisms are held to be of sovereign efficacy for
happiness."[4] The first part of the Doctrines is
a group of four statements which summarizes the most
important concepts of the philosophy. These were
caled by the ancient Greeks the **tetrapharmakon**. The
word is difficult to translate because it implies
an all-purpose remedy consisting of beeswax, resin,
pitch, and honey. A "four-compound" patent medicine
might be a modern interpretation of the word. There
is an implication of ridicule associated with the
name, which was given by detractors to show how
Epicureans accepted the words of the Master as a
type of Doctor's medicine.

The **tetrapharmakon** proclaims that there is nothing
to fear from the serene and blessed gods; that death
is nothing to be feared; that pleasure exists whenever
pain is absent; that pain can be easily overcome.
These were the Epicurean Articles of Faith and they
introduced the topics which a new learner would spend
the remainder of his life applying in his personal
conduct.

From the quotation previously given from Cicero,
as well as a reference in Diogenes Laertius, it is
known that Epicurus' associates committed his writings
to memory. In the New England, the middle, and
southern colonies of seventeenth and eighteenth century
America the first instructional aids were hornbooks
and battledores. These were, in effect, handbooks
to introduce small children to the catechism of the

church. Later the youth would move on to longer books like the <u>New England Primer</u>, which provided a detailed account of the orthodox faith. The <u>Principal Doctrines</u> of Epicurus served the raw recruits for the Garden in the same fashion as the hornbook and battledore in early American schools.

Unquestionably there were additional primary level instructional aids in Epicurus' school of which we have no record. Perhaps several of the informative letters, like those written to Herodotus, Pythocles, and Menoeceus were required reading and subject to memorization by the students. Since Epicurus advised his disciples to dwell on the doctrines "night and day" in order to grow in spiritual understanding, there was a great deal of study, reflection, and memorization before a student would feel he had mastered all Epicurean knowledge.

An indication of the value of books to Epicurean study is the fact that during the late Roman period and early Middle Ages when Christian emperors and leaders tried to eradicate the pagan religions and philosophies, they set about destroying the books. In this way they dealt a serious blow to the Epicurean school because it had always relied to a significant degree on publications which specifically spelled out the dogma of the Garden. This is one reason the Epicurean philosophy declined as a major cult during the early Middle Ages.

EDUCATION AS RECREATION

It would appear from the memorization and reading required for followers of the Master that the academic life of the Garden was a drudgery of unceasing intellectual toil. Throughout most of human history where rote learning and extensive reading have been required for mastery of school subjects, the academic climate has not been filled with joy. In the Garden, however, the case was different. Pleasure was the key to the academic program and the **schole** of Epicurus was truly an institution devoted to the pursuit of truth in leisure. Diogenes Laertius assures his readers that to Epicurus education was synonymous with "recreation." Students did not sit long hours in wooden desks arduously pursuing studies which they disliked. Quite the contrary, the leisurely pursuit of Epicurean wisdom in play and recreation was the format.

TRAINING IN SELF-DISCOVERY

Unlike training for ancient Greek Olympic sports competition, where athletes were required to develop the body and physical skills under the close direction of a coach, tutelage in the Garden was very informal. The Olympic competitor was trained according to specific rules under close supervision, while, in contrast, those students developing strength of mind and character in the Garden were allowed great latitude in their training. Epicurus understood that the search for enlightenment was often a lonely vigil in which friends could offer aid and encouragement, but the ultimate decision-making and progress depended on individual effort.

The Master, although the leader of friends living a communal life, recognized that ultimately each man stands alone when attempting to discover and realize his true nature. Friends can help, but, as he stated, "Approval from others must come unasked, while we seek to improve the conditions of our own lives."[5] Whereas some religions teach the guardian relationship between God and man, stressing the need for man to achieve self-realization in accepting the dictates of a holy spirit, Epicurus said, "It is ridiculous to pray to the gods for help, when a man is capable of providing for himself."[6]

Training for self-realization at Epicurus' school was an individual experience, aided by the words of the Master, encouraged by the help of friends, and achieved by individual effort. In Buddhist religion the process is known as the search for enlightenment. Buddhism, which is actually a philosophy of life rather than a religion controlled by a theistic deity, teaches a creed very similar in some ways to Epicureanism. Both belief systems recognize the danger of unnecessary and unnatural desires which can inhibit full realization of the goal of enlightened happiness. Buddhists (like Epicureans with their **tetrapharmakon**) accept "Four Noble Truths" which are stated as follows:

56

1. Existence is unhappiness.
2. Unhappiness is caused by selfish craving.
3. Selfish craving can be defeated.
4. It can be defeated by following the eightfold path.

Epicureans believed human existence, for the mass of men in society, was unhappy. They shared the Buddist belief that unhappiness is caused by craving selfish desires and that those desires can be destroyed. Even some of the steps on the "eightfold path" such as: right understanding, right purpose, right speech, and right conduct were necessary actions to arrive at Epicurean happiness. When a Buddhist teacher says that happiness is found in transcending our selfish craving and, therefore, following the path to enlightenment, he means the self-realization and discovery which was close to the aim of the Garden. Of course, there are features of the metaphysics and epistemology of Buddhism, as well as some axiological principles, which are alien to Epicureanism. For instance, the idea of reincarnation and the influence of Karma on the afterlife are completely different from the philosophy of Epicurus, but both schools of thought sought **ataraxia** through self-discovery.

Since peace of mind was the aim of the students at the Garden (in much the same way that Buddhist students seek mental serenity) the achievement of this educational goal was obvious to the learner when it was found. In Buddhism the result is **Nirvana**, in Epicureanism the result was the "serenity of the gods." **Ataraxia**, as an educational goal, is difficult to achieve, but the final realization is obvious. Where students at the Academy of Plato were assumed to possess the qualities of a philosopher-king at age thirty-five, and students of rhetoric in the school of Isocrates were assumed to be capable orators when they graduated; Epicureans, like Buddhists, knew with certainty that in Epicurus' words, "The man who is tranquil disturbs neither himself nor anyone else."[7] When the self-realization of **ataraxia** was achieved it was obvious and unquestioned.

TRUST IN PERSONAL JUDGMENT

Where a student of music, grammar, rhetoric,

and other studies could never arrive at perfect knowledge, the Epicurean, setting his sight upon achieving only **eudaemonia via ataraxia**, was fortunate. Serenity is self-proclaiming, whereas all other fields of endeavor offer only partial fulfillment. Students of the Master were taught that achievement of the blessed state of **eudaemonia** was not measured by a standard imposed by society; to enjoy the fruits of **ataraxia** was a personal experience very difficult to share with others. Evaluating the attainment of the condition required individual assessment and trust in personal judgment.

Today in formal education the progress of a student's work is made by teachers who evaluate performance on report cards. Since most schools in the United States rely on appraisal based on performance norms established by local school districts and state law, comparison of student achievement against a specific standard allows objective-type grading. This was impossible in the Epicurean school. Performance at a level to indicate successful fulfillment of the educational goal of the Garden was made possible only by the student **himself** or **herself** judging if life was happy and the mind serene.

In addition, each student acquired personal awareness of success in finding **eudaemonia via ataraxia** by leading a life that in outward appearance might not reveal his competency. Successful mathematicians can prove their ability by performing prodigious physical feats, but Epicureans could only prove their success by the self-confidence of personal knowledge. Therefore, a report card in the Garden had to be written by the student evaluating his own educational progress.

Epicurus recognized that his students would have to trust to personal judgment of their progress in achieving the goal of his educational system. For this reason he offered personal views on character attributes which the "wise man," (one who had achieved **ataraxia**) would possess. Fortunately, in Diogenes Laertius' Lives, a record exists of some of the examples of the character of the "wise man." The Epicurean would:

....Feel gratitude towards friends, present and absent alike, and show it by word and deed.

The wise man will not make fine speeches.

Nor will he punish his servants. . . .

Nor, again, will the wise man marry and rear
a family. . . .[8]

Many other attributes of behavior for the "wise
man" were listed by Diogenes Laertius, including
the admonition that a man shouldn't become a tyrant,
nor become a mendicant, nor engage in sexual
indulgence, nor ruin his reputation by questionable
acts.

Such suggestions were signs for the Epicurean
recruit to follow in his evaluation of the personal
criteria for conduct. Unlike the Principal Doctrines,
which were specific statements dogmatically imposed
on his students, Epicurus' suggestions for the wise
man were only helpful aids to assist the disciple
in determining whether his progress was in conformity
to normal Epicurean conduct. However, many of the
resident-members of the Garden achieved **eudaemonia
via ataraxia** in contradiction to the Master's
suggestions.

Metrodorus, for one, ignored the recommendation
that a man should not marry by taking the hetaira
Leontion as his wife and raising a family. In fact,
his daughter Danae later became a Greek heroine
when she sacrificed her life (in good Epicurean
fashion) for her lover's safety in Ephesus.
Metrodorus, as Epicurus' closest friend and an
Associate Leader at the Garden, evidently believed
marriage and family did not hinder successful arrival
at the goal of Epicurean **eudaemonia**.

It is likely there were other numerous examples
of "wise men" arriving at happiness through peace
of mind who did not conform in all features to the
personality and character of Epicurus. In other
words, nonconformity, as long as the aim of Epicurean
education was realized, was acceptable at the Garden.
Personal judgment about many aspects of life was
allowed and individuality was encouraged: free
will and freedom to develop an individual life style
were choices which encouraged every student to learn
and think for himself. The student in the Garden
was required to trust in personal judgment on all
axiological questions.

TRAINING FOR CRITICAL THINKING

Where students accepted the physical science principles of Epicurus without question, and adhered to the rigidity of his metaphysical and epistemological philosophical foundations, the approach to axiology was an entirely different matter. Certain injunctions served as guidelines for action, but most friends of the Garden used personal judgment in the conduct of everyday life. In order to prepare students for the freedom of choice to learn and apply the tenets of Epicurean happiness in their personal lives, it was necessary to develop the ability for critical thinking.

Critical thinking for the Epicurean was using logic without slavishly following the specific rules for logic study as developed in the traditional Greek school. For this reason Epicurus did not approve of logic as a curricular subject, rather his students worked to develop powers of systematic inquiry into problem solving. Unfortunately, unlike the Dialogues of Plato and Xenophon which show the educational methodology of Socrates, no literature exists to detail the technique Epicurus used to train his students in critical thinking.

One fragment remains which relates a conversation between Polyaenus and the Master of the Garden discussing the change in body temperature and feeling caused by wine. This short dialogue offers little insight into the methods of Epicurean pedagogical instruction, however, it opens the door for speculation on one aspect of critical thinking. Unquestionably, conversation between friends at the school helped students develop the ability to reason in a logical and systematic manner. Philosophical debate between resident-members offered each student the opportunity to acquire precision in thinking about the alternatives for self-directed effort.

Epicurus believed emphatically that dialogue and discourse were necessary for training the young mind in the principles of critical thinking. The Master once said that the person who is defeated in philosophical debate gains more than the winner,

60

insofar as he learns more. This point of view enabled students to enter the arena of debate without trepidation that their ideas would be met with derision and scorn. Practice in debate at the Garden, unlike Plato's Academy, did not place a high premium on using the dialectic approach as an end in itself, rather the Garden avoided competitive training in logic, rhetoric, and dialectic to encourage the development of critical thinking as the only aid in spiritual salvation.

Critical thinking to Epicurus was an approach to philosophy using theoretical reasoning without adherence to rigid rules of logic; it was an important step in the training of young minds because it disciplined the student to respect the difference between an inference based on myth or superstition, and one based on evidential authority. Once the follower of Epicurus mastered the skills of reasoning on a theoretical basis he was able to defend the ethical theory of happiness by logical deduction. Skilled philosophers, defending their creed in the arena of argumentation and debate, were necessary in ancient Greece. Only through the influence of those teachers of the art of persuasion could new members be attracted to the Garden and other schools.

PRUDENCE AND THE DICTATES OF REASON

Although critical thinking and the development of practitioners of logic was important to the Garden it was recognized that such instruction would not avail the average man on the street. Epicurus wanted his philosophy to be available to everyone seeking happiness and peace of mind. "O wretched minds of men! O hearts of darkness!" sang the poet Lucretius when he called for all desperate and unhappy men to turn to Epicurus. Since barbarians, slaves, and courtesans (among others) joined the Garden, the Master recognized that training in the techniques of critical thinking would offer difficulty to some students and be of questionable value to most. For this reason he placed all training in theoretical subjects in second place to educating his students to use common sense.

Plato and Aristotle enthroned pure or theoretical reason as the capstone of philosophy. In the

61

<u>Nicomachean Ethics</u>, Aristotle suggests that practical wisdom is important, but not as important as what he termed philosophic wisdom. Pure or theoretical reason was called philosophic wisdom by the ancient Greeks and they distinguished this from **phronesis**, which was practical wisdom, right judgment, sober calculation, or prudence. When the Academy of Plato trained students to develop philosophical or pure reason as the highest goal, the Garden of Epicurus did the opposite. It is not surprising that Plato, the rationalist, would stress pure reason while Epicurus, the empiricist, would stress practical wisdom. The philosophy of idealism, introduced by Plato, strives to define the unchanging reality of a perfect universe where "forms" or "models" or "ideals" provide the only true permanencies. The philosophy of Epicurus, grounded in the cold realism of empirical fact, scoffed at the theoretical conditions proposed by the Socratics and turned to a materialistic world defined by practical wisdom.

Garden students sought to achieve self-realization and spiritual salvation through critical thinking and **phronesia**. Prudence, good judgment, or practical reasoning (although scholars use many definitions for **phronesia**, the word "prudence" is being used here) became the proof for Epicurus that his egoistic hedonism was a philosophy of benefit to society as well as to the individual. Evidently the Master was sensitive to criticism that his students were working to achieve a mental state of happiness which was inimical to the general welfare of Greek society. For this reason he proposed that virtuous action in life, which is necessary for the benefit of mankind, results from a prudent living pattern. Living virtuously is the same as living prudently, which is the same as living pleasantly. Each is dependent upon one another and the result is advantageous to the individual and society.

> It is impossible to live pleasantly without living prudently, well, and justly, (and to live prudently, well, and justly) without living pleasantly. Even though a man lives well and justly, it is not possible for him to live pleasantly if he lacks that from which stems the prudent life.[9]

The previous quotation, which was listed as the fifth <u>Principal Doctrine</u> of Epicurus, shows the Greek teacher's concern for encouraging his students to recognize the relationship between living a life of pleasure, and of virtuous conduct. For the Master, pleasure which led to happiness, tempered by prudent judgment, had to result in just and virtuous ends. Justice and righteousness always followed as a result of seeking pleasure through prudence. Diogenes Laertius reports that, "Epicurus describes virtue as the **sine qua non** of pleasure, i.e., the one thing without which pleasure cannot be. . . ."[10]

A detailed explanation of prudence and the need for each student to strive to develop his full potential to apply **phronesis** in every aspect of life is found in the Letter to Menoeceus. In this letter Epicurus advises his student that **philosophia** (theoretical wisdom) is not as important as **phronesis** (prudence) which teaches that the virtues of the just life are inseparably tied to the pleasures of Epicurean life. The Master notes that by using prudence a man will be able to choose those advantages which will allow him to find the happiness of **ataraxia**.

Theoretical speculation and the intricacies of epistemological and axiological abstractions were unnecessary for the average Epicurean student because they did not serve to improve the condition of life, and Epicurus insisted that the philosopher's word is useless if it does not contribute to healing the sufferings of mankind. There was no doubt, however, about the practical necessity for prudence in healing suffering. By training his students to weigh the advantages of one course of action taken, the Master suggested that chance or fortune was alleviated and the prudent man was in control of his own destiny. In fact, one of the Principal Doctrines, number sixteen, states, "Chance rarely troubles a wise man. Prudence directs and controls the essential things, and continues to direct them throughout a man's life."[11]

Students at the Garden were instructed to apply common sense in every situation where a choice of conduct was available, because prudence was a practical skill necessary for all men to develop. Theoretical logic and critical thinking were important in understanding the rationale for cult dogma, but prudence armed a man with the best weapon to fight fate, fortune, and chance. The person of good judgment always chooses wisely and virtuously and this leads to the pleasant life of **eudaemonia via ataraxia**, suggested the Greek teacher. By the example of prudent teachers and the experience of decision-making the students in the Garden cultivated **phronesis**, the capstone of Epicurean ethics.

GRATITUDE AND RESPECT FOR OTHERS

Individuality and uniqueness of character were traits which the Epicurean school cultivated with its training for self-realization, trust in personal judgment, encouragement of critical thinking, and the use of prudence. The aim of Garden education was to develop a capable, self-reliant, and happy person. In his curricular plan Epicurus promoted independence for the individual, and yet he never forgot that in a society one must be attentive to the needs of others. This was best expressed in friendship, which became the most suitable educational device for moving from a purely egoistic and selfish conduct of life to a responsibility for the welfare of others.

Adjustment to society, which is sometimes listed as an aim of public education today, was unimportant in the sheltered utopia of the Garden. Epicurean philosophy turned to the cultivation of individual excellence and completely ignored Athenian life. With his renunciation of third century B.C. Greek society, Epicurus taught an educational theory which supported salvation of spirit for the individual and respect for the rights of others. This dichotomy of purpose meant that an impetuous and headstrong egoistic hedonist soon discovered that regardless of his uniqueness and individuality, he had a responsibility to respect and serve his associates. Altruism with a social service motive was not the reason that a student in the Garden had to be aware of others and consider their welfare, rather it was because personal happiness cannot be achieved without sharing pleasure with others.

Epicurus remarked, "That also is very beautiful, the sight of those near and dear to us, when to the ties of blood is joined a union of hearts; for such a sight is a great help to intimacy."[12] **Eudaemonia** in the Garden was a personal serenity of spirit complimented by the love and support of faithful friends. The relationship between friends in the Garden was close enough to have them be "of one mind." In such an environment the students willingly worked to please their friends and, in return, gratitude was given.

Greeks felt gratitude to their city-state for protection, to their parents for nurture, and to their friends for enriching and making their lives happier. Gratitude is a familiar theme in Epicurean writing and it appears that it ranked with prudence among the highest of Garden virtues. The Master insisted that a wise man, "will be grateful to anyone when he is corrected."[13] The educational implications of this statement are obvious. Faculty members, as well as students in the Garden, would not have hesitated to acknowledge criticism and correction as important educational devices. By specific mention of the gratitude one should show for correction, there is little doubt that criticism was encouraged and a necessary component to educational methodology at the school.

Diogenes Laertius quotes the Greek teacher as advising every Epicurean that, "He alone will feel gratitude towards friends, present and absent alike, and show it by word and deed."[14] Doubtless, this applied to students who needed to show gratitude to teachers for assistance in discovering the path to Epicurean enlightenment. The resident-members of the Garden were conditioned to feel and show an obligation to serve one another respectfully at all times. In making such a definitive statement about feeling gratitude and showing it by word and deed the Master united the communal society and made each member responsible for the welfare of others.

Epicurus placed an especially high premium on gratitude to family members. In Lives, Diogenes Laertius relates, ". . . .his gratitude to his parents, his generosity to his brothers, his gentleness to his servants. . . ."[15] Provisions in the will of Epicurus, found in the same source, also describe in detail the gratitude and generosity of the founder of the Garden. This evidence, along with other sources from antiquity, indicate Epicurus practiced what he preached. Ironically, however, he would not show gratitude toward his own teachers. Epicurus refused to pay tribute to the teachers he read and studied with during his youth, insisting

65

that he was self-educated.

TEACHING AS TOTAL LIVING

Faculty members at the Garden, such as:
Metrodorus, Hermarchus, Polyaenus, Leontion, and
Epicurus' brothers did not work a normal routine
for a teacher in antiquity; let alone like the
schedule of work for an educator living in
twentieth-century America. Teaching was not a
nine-to-four o'clock occupation, five days a week
for thirty-six weeks of the year. Quite the contrary,
it was a total life commitment every hour of every
day. Education at the Garden was a full-time activity
requiring the faculty to participate in the
living-learning environment day and night, whenever
their services were needed. Since the associate
and assistant leaders were teachers who ministered
to the souls of their students, they were, by
necessity, available at all times and, hence, had
almost no private lives. Privateness was at odds
with the school of which Epicurus said, "You should
do nothing in your life that will cause you fear
should it become known to those who live around
you."[16] Life in the Epicurean community was an
open book, with members having no secrets from one
another, in fact, secretiveness was viewed as the
one element most destructive to Epicurean friendship.

CANDOR AND HONESTY

To insure open and honest relationships at
his school Epicurus insisted on complete candor.
It was felt that the most injurious factor in
friendship was furtive, deceitful ideas which were
not spoken openly. The brotherhood of the Garden
learned to accept criticism and constructive
suggestions from faculty and students alike, so
there was no reason for friendships to dissolve
over censorious words. The Master was a dogmatist
and he condemned those who were unwilling to take
a stand on an issue and defend it; for this reason
he found fault with students who were unwilling
to be frank and honest in their opinions.

66

One of the most famous stories of antiquity is the visit of Chaerephon to the Oracle at Delphi, where the question was asked if anyone was wiser than Socrates. When the priestess replied, "No one," Chaerephon returned to his teacher Socrates seeking the philosopher's reaction. Athenaeus states that Socrates answered by completely "disowning wisdom for himself." This popular story must have been familiar to Epicurus because he accused Socrates of dishonesty and a lack of candidness in his answer. Socrates was not only intelligent and knowledgeable, but he knew it in his own heart, yet told his students otherwise. Epicurus reminded his followers that the good man is always honest and forthright about his knowledge and abilities. The Master advised his students that, ". . . .he who has once become wise never more assumes the opposite habit, not even in semblance, if he can help it."[17]

Candor was so important to Epicurean ethics that students in the Garden were advised to always speak openly and honestly even if they were not understood, and even if the results would be indignation from the mass of men. Epicurus explained this concept in the following way:

> When studying nature count on me to speak
> candidly, like an oracle, giving answers helpful
> to all men. Rather than give public opinions
> to win the plaudits of the crowd, I will utter
> truths even though no one should listen or
> understand me.[18]

Candor and honesty in human relations gives the immediate appearance that the Epicureans were harsh and aggressively forthright in their criticism of themselves and others. It is true they spoke openly and to the point, but it was done with a gentleness and kindness which removed the sting from their bold speech.

GENTLE FRIEND AND CONFIDANT

History has portrayed Epicurus in many images, he has been a saint to some and a sinner to other observers; his philosophy has been condemned and his educational system reviled. Little agreement is found among commentators during 2300 years of criticism. In one area, however, there is unanimous agreement: by every historical account Epicurus had a gentle and kind personality. In fact, a popular assessment, which probably originated from a member of the Epicurean school, was, "Epicurus' life when compared to other men's in respect of gentleness and self-sufficiency might be thought a mere .legend."[19] Diogenes Laertius remarks about the, "abundance of witnesses to attest his unsurpassed goodwill to all men. . . ."[20]

Epicurus represented the ideal of a gentle friend and confidant. Since all faculty members at the Garden followed his lead, the harshness and aggressiveness of candid speech was ameliorated by the gentle love exhibited to all students. The leader of the Athenian school became a confidant, guide, and loving friend to his disciples - he was candid, but fair in a fatherly way. Therefore, the Master offered psychological and emotional help to his friends, as well as intellectual guidance; other faculty members were expected to provide succor to troubled minds and bodies in the same way as the leader of the Garden.

An expression used in the field of education for hundreds of years, **in loco parentis** (in the place of a parent), perhaps best describes the position of a faculty member at the Epicurean school. Reference has already been made to the example of a family relationship at the Garden. The importance of this analogy cannot be underestimated. All evidence, from the writings of Epicurus to the opinions of generations of observers, points to the fact that the Garden represented the close **philia** relationship of parents and children. The Master was unmarried and childless and, in fact, advised against marriage and raising a family. Even so, Epicurus possessed a deep love and feeling of responsibility for the welfare of children. Fragments from his writings refer to children with kindness expressed in the most effusive language. In his will particular mention is made of children and he commands his followers to care for the son and daughter of Metrodorus and the son of Polyaenus.

One does not have to be a parent to express a fondness and love for children. Since more than half of the three page last will and testament Epicurus wrote went into great detail about the schooling, dowry for marriage, property settlement, and trust fund to be established for his friends' children, it is obvious the Master showed a great concern for young people. In a warm and very loving note to a little girl Epicurus revealed the tenderness and affection of a doting older friend.

> I hope you are well, too, and your mamma, and
> that you obey her and papa and Matron in
> everything, as you used to do. For you know
> quite well, my pet, that I and all the others
> love you very much, because you are obedient
> to them in everything.[21]

The Vatican Collection of Epicurean fragments offer testimony to the importance of gentle love necessary for living with children. As a teacher and parent-substitute for his students, Epicurus outlined clearly the steps to be taken in dealing with the young. First, gentleness was necessary. Anger directed at children, he suggested, was unnecessary. One quote exists in which the Greek teacher worried about intruding into the parents' relationship with their young, yet at the same time felt it necessary to advise proper handling of the youngsters.

> If the anger of parents against their children
> is justified, it is quite foolish for the children
> to resist it and to fail to seek forgiveness. If
> the anger is justified but is unreasonable, it
> is folly for a child to increase the unreasoning
> wrath by his own anger and not try to turn it
> aside in other directions by a display of good
> feeling.[22]

As a gentle and loving father-confessor, Epicurus always opposed the use of anger in human affairs. Seneca is quoted as stating that Epicurus believed uncontrolled anger "leads to madness."

Since he believed anger must be replaced by gentleness in dealing with students, Epicurus and his faculty established a rule of love at the Garden. As in the case of most families, the brotherhood of the Epicurean school was taught from the motivation of love. It has already been mentioned that **philia**, the word for friendship used by Epicurus, can also be translated as love. Therefore when Epicurus said "Philia goes dancing through the world bidding us to awake and give praises to the happy life,"[23] the Master meant both love and friendship are necessary for **eudaemonia**.

By being a gentle friend and confidant a teacher at the Garden showed the love of a parent. This parental concern for spiritual welfare of the students was one reason the school prospered for hundreds of years. In direct refutation of educational practice in many Athenian and Spartan schools, where schoolmasters exacted severe discipline through heavy physical punishment, the Epicureans taught by the example of kindness and gentleness. **In loco parentis**, to Epicurus, was an educational concept meaning to bring the love of a family into the school.

EDUCATION BY EMULATION

The care and concern of the Epicurean family for the welfare of the resident-members of the Garden was exemplified in the close attention which the faculty paid to their young charges. Since the concern of the teachers was to help the students grow in self-realization and self-sufficiency, avoiding the pitfalls of unnecessary desires and vain pursuits, it was necessary to set the best possible example. Epicurus outlined the task for teachers when he stated, "The first step to self-realization is to watch over young people, and to protect them against anything which causes trouble by means of tempting desires."[24] By watching over the students, teachers set the stage for showing the young men and women how to find **eudaemonia via ataraxia**. The search was an individual endeavor, but gentle faculty friends offered a wealth of educational aids in the pursuit of Epicurean truth.

Books, lectures, kindly admonition, and spirited debate highlighted the educational process, but the best means of discovering the path to wisdom was by observation and imitation of the successful Epicureans. Students learned in the Garden by emulating their leaders. One person stood as a perfect example for students to observe. That, of course, was Epicurus. Reference has been made on numerous occasions to the veneration and respect which was shown to the Master. His friends in the Garden wished to imitate his behavior and share the perfect composure and peace of mind which

70

exemplified the highest character of Epicureanism.

A teacher in the Garden was worthy of respect and admiration because he had arrived at the Epicurean truth of **eudaemonia via ataraxia**, and in the daily conduct of his life he exhibited the high character which each student sought to imitate. Seneca, the Roman Stoic teacher and essayist, understood this idea and he referred to the necessity of emulating a wise man in one of his moral epistles. In Epistle XI to Lucilius, Seneca tells a friend to imitate the counsel of the Epicureans by taking a man of high character, one worthy of singular respect, and revering this model to such a degree that he is ever "before your eyes;" living in such a way that you feel his eyes always upon you. Seneca, who wrote paternalistically to Lucilius, very likely thought of himself as the man of high character whom Lucilius should admire and keep in his thoughts. There is no question that at the Garden Epicurus and his faculty were the ideal and standard for the students to revere and imitate.

PLAIN LANGUAGE IN PUBLISHING

In addition to serving as emulatory models for the resident-students in the Garden, faculty members published extensively in hopes of reaching perspective candidates for Epicureanism outside of the school. The Master was one of the most prolific writers in the ancient world with over three hundred books (scrolls) to his credit. Associate leaders like Metrodorus and Hermarchus also published; the former credited with twenty books; the latter recognized as author of more than twenty-five books.

The voluminous output by Epicurus and his friends must have kept faculty and students busy writing and reading one another's works. Unfortunately with this wealth of Epicurean publications, which would serve to enlighten the modern scholar on many features of the school, almost nothing remains today. During the Christian era of the early Middle Ages nearly all Epicurean books were destroyed because of their pagan content.

In evaluating the existing fragmented writings

of the Epicureans evidence points to simplicity of speech and plain language as a characteristic. Diogenes Laertius reports that the expressions which Epicurus used "were the ordinary terms" and that he made "clearness the sole requisite" for writing. Therefore ease of understanding was the first consideration in publication. The resident-members of the Garden wrote in a simple language, easily understood by the common man. Doubtless this is one reason why converts from all social classes and educational levels joined the cult; the dogma and creed of Epicureanism were easy to understand. No interpretative difficulties are found among the extant remains of Epicurus' writing. Compared to Plato and Aristotle, both of whom wrote abstract and obtuse treatises, the leader of the Garden outlined his axiology in specific, nontechnical terms.

CHAPTER IV

HISTORICAL COMMENT AND APPRAISAL

During the Hellenistic and early Roman period one school, Stoicism, offered the major challenge to the dominance of the Epicureans for philosophical supremacy in the Mediterranean world. For two hundred years following the death of Epicurus, until the start of the Roman Empire, each school vied for students in a competition which was at times intense and bitter. The shifting political machinations of the Roman Republic and Empire provided periods when first one, then the other philosophy, prospered and gained ascendancy in the minds of men. Stoicism commonly appealed to the aristocracy, whereas Epicureanism became popular among the poor and middle class, particularly in towns and rural areas.

The parallel history of these two Greek schools which so greatly influenced Roman Civilization had its beginning in third century B.C. Athens. While Epicurus was exhorting his friends in the Garden on the outskirts of Athens, Zeno, a native of Citium in Cyprus, was lecturing at the Painted Stoa in the Agora of Athens. Zeno, as a student of Crates (Diogenes' most famous pupil), was educated in the Cynic School. He developed his own ideas, parted company with the Cynics, and gained adherents called Stoics - named for the Stoa where he paced up and down lecturing to anyone who would listen. Zeno (followed by Cleanthes, who was followed by Chrysippus as leaders in the School) developed the dogma which

became the Stoic philosophy. Although the rivalry
between the followers of Zeno and Epicurus became
intense in later generations, especially under the
influence of Chrysippus who wrote several diatribes
against the Garden, there was no initial hostility
between the philosophies. We do not know what the
Master thought about Zeno's sect, but two of his
closest friends, Colotes and Polyaenus, were friendly
rather than hostile to the Stoics.

A number of theoretical features in the
philosophy of the Porch (another name for Stoicism)
differed in considerable degree to the teachings
of the Garden School. Stoics accepted the Platonic
notion of the immortality of the soul, although
they did not believe in the theory of "Ideas," or
"Forms." They used code words such as "duty" and
"service" to describe the responsibility one has
to honor one's parents, friends, and country.
Epicurus, likewise, felt a duty to serve friends
and relatives, but he differed from the Stoics on
the issue of civic service. One of the most important
spokesmen for the ethics of Zeno's philosophy was
the Roman essayist Seneca. In his <u>Moral Essays</u>
Seneca points out the differences between Stoicism
and Epicureanism on the issue of public affairs:

> The two sects, the Epicureans and the Stoics,
> are at variance, as in most things, in this matter
> also; they both direct us to leisure, but by
> different roads. Epicurus says: 'The wise man
> will not engage in public affairs except in an
> emergency.' Zeno says: 'He will engage in
> public affairs unless something prevents him.'[1]

The suggestion of Seneca that the two sects
were at variance on most issues is not totally
accurate. The schools were characterized by differing
views on metaphysics, particularly in theology,
but basically they shared the same position on ethics.
Virtue and happiness were important to followers
of both the Porch and the Garden. Stoics believed
that happiness would result from having virtue as
the **summum bonum** of life, while Epicurus taught
that by seeking and finding happiness, it would
be necessary to follow the virtuous life.
Disagreement between the Schools was on which came
first as the ultimate aim of human conduct - virtue
or happiness. This difference was often mentioned
in the writings of Stoic philosophers during Roman
times; Epictetus, for one, suggested in his writings

that Epicureans were little better than "debauchees" because they advocated happiness (which the Stoic interpreted as pleasure) as the **summum bonum**, instead of virtuous conduct which was promoted as the ultimate aim by the followers of Zeno. The argument over the first principle of ethical behavior between the schools was more a matter of semantic contention than an important philosophical distinction. Actually, Epictetus and his Stoic colleagues were quibbling because the ethical position of the two Roman schools was very similar and the philosophers of the Porch were overeager in seeking philosophical points of departure.

Epictetus, who lived from approximately 50 A.D. to 120 A.D., was much admired as a writer by Stoics such as the Emperor Marcus Aurelius, and early Christians like Chrysostom, Augustine, and Origen. His philosophy, published from the stenographic notes recorded by his student Arrian, provides scholars with the most detailed exposition of the philosophy of the Porch. There is an amazing similarity in language between Epicurus and Epictetus, particularly on the subject of **ataraxia**. The Stoic teacher advised, "It is better to die of hunger, but in a state of freedom from grief and fear, than to live in plenty, but troubled in mind."[2] These were exactly the sentiments of Epicurus, nearly four hundred years earlier, when he wrote, "It is better for you to be free of fear lying upon a bed of straw, than to have a golden couch and a rich table and be full of trouble."[3] In discussing the theme of **ataraxia**, Epictetus also provided the following maxims:

> Fortify yourself with contentment; for this is an impregnable fortress.[4]

> If you are maintaining the character of a man of tranquillity, of imperturbability, of sedateness .... if you are not envying those who are preferred in honour above you, if the mere subject-matter of actions does not dazzle you, what do you lack?[5]

> Men, if you heed me, wherever you may be, whatever you may be doing, you will feel no pain, no anger, no compulsion, no hindrance, but you will pass your lives in tranquillity and in freedom from every disturbance.[6]

> It is difficult, I own, to blend and unite tranquillity

75

in accepting, and energy in using, the facts of
life; but it is not impossible; if it be, it is
impossible to be happy.[7]

Ataraxia for Epictetus and the Stoic teachers
was rooted in the world of science and reason;
controlled by an inflexible law of nature. Rational
conduct was connected to the determinist idea of
destiny over which man had no control, therefore
the Stoics accepted the dictates of nature with
forbearance and **ataraxia**. The man of tranquillity
was advised to use rational conduct and accept any
contingency without flinching. Since fortitude
in the face of adversity was accepted as a manifest
destiny by the Stoics, they refused to accept the
pleasure principle of hedonism. Although there
were differences between the philosophy of the Porch
and the School of Epicurus many themes
(self-realization, self-sufficiency, friendship,
abstemiousness, prudence and **ataraxia**) wove a similar
axiological pattern through the Roman creeds.

EPICURUS AND THE CHRISTIANS

During the Roman Empire the philosophies of
Stoicism and Epicureanism drew much closer. In
fact, by the time Marcus Aurelius wrote his
Meditations as a testament to the teachings of the
Porch he had incorporated as much Epicureanism as
Stoicism in his treatise. The philosophical opponent
which caused the decline in fortunes for both schools
was Christianity. With a tenacious hold on the
minds of people throughout the Mediterranean world,
from Asia Minor to North Africa to Spain, the Garden
outlived most other Greek philosophical systems,
but it could not withstand the sweep of the Christian
movement which eventually caused the demise of the
Master's school late in the fourth century A.D.
After that time little was heard about the teachings
of Epicurus because almost all Christian theologians
chose to ignore pagan creeds.

Through his influence on two writers of the
Bible, however, Epicurus left an impact on
Christianity which remains to this day. First,
one of the books of the Old Testament, Ecclesiastes,
very likely was written by a member of the Garden
School (or, at least, a philosopher with Epicurean

76

sympathies).   The   second   impact   on   Christianity
was the Epicurean flavor of the New Testament Letters
written by St. Paul.

Ecclesiastes was written by a Hebrew philosopher
who   was   attempting   to   impersonate   King   Solomon.
Although inconsistent in the advocacy of Epicurean
dogma, there exist numerous sections of Ecclesiastes
which exemplify the teachings of the Garden.   Such
admonitions as the following suggest the influence
of Epicurus on the author of the Old Testament book.

> I know that there is nothing good for man except
> to be happy and live the best life he can while
> he is alive.[8]

> The man who loves money can never have enough,
> and the man who is in love with great wealth
> enjoys no return from it.[9]

> It is better to be satisfied with what is before
> your eyes than give rein to desire; this too is
> emptiness and chasing the wind.[10]

> So I commend enjoyment, since there is nothing
> good for a man to do here under the sun but to
> eat and drink and enjoy himself.[11]

> But for a man who is counted among the living
> there is still hope: remember, a live dog is better
> than a dead lion. True, the living know that they
> will die; but the dead know nothing.[12]

> Banish discontent from your mind, and shake off the
> troubles of the body; boyhood and the prime of life
> are mere emptiness.[13]

> One further warning, my son: the use of books
> is endless, and much study is wearisome.[14]

Where several of the sentiments of Ecclesiastes
are found in other parts of the Bible, the Hebrew
author of this book addresses himself to themes
not found elsewhere.   For instance, the fifth
quotation strongly suggests the author did not believe
in immortality of the soul.   The sixth quotation
voices the same refrain as the Vatican Collection
fragment number XVII in which Epicurus states, "We
should not think of a young man as being happy,
but rather the old man who has lived a good life."[15]
In   addition,   the   last   quotation   issues   the   same

warning against traditional, formal education which was voiced by Epicurus. Other sections of the Old Testament book - Chapter IV on the value of friendship and Chapter VI advocating the simple life - acknowledge a debt to the Garden.

There is no question that Epicureanism made inroads in Judea and the Near East. The author of Ecclesiastes might have studied at one of many schools teaching the Greek philosophy. One influential Epicurean center was located at Antioch, and through the influence of this school, which enjoyed the patronage of Antiochus Epiphanes and his successor, the doctrine of the Master became familiar to all educated men living in the area. This included Paul of Tarsus - St. Paul of the New Testament. Several scholars have offered the thesis that St. Paul was not only familiar with the Garden philosophy, but influenced by Epicureanism when he drafted the Pauline Epistles. Internal appraisal of the New Testament Letters indicates innumerable parallels between the writing of the Christian popularizer and the earlier work of the Master of the Garden.

THE CHRISTIAN CONDEMNATION

St. Paul appears to have had a grudging respect for Epicurus, but later Christians either ignored or condemned all the teachings of the Master. Because of the belief in deism rather than monotheism, and the rejection of the immortal soul, the Epicureans were denounced by the church as the prototype atheistic pagans. The most famous example of this point of view is found in the Medieval classic Divina Commedia (Divine Comedy) written by Dante Alighieri. The poem offers the view that in the sixth circle of Hell, Epicurus and his followers receive, for eternity, the judgment due to heretics. Using symbolic and colorful language, with a vicious horrific effect, Dante has the Epicureans suffering where flames lash out making "iron red-hot." Ironically, Dante's literary leader for his tour of Hell is Virgil, a Roman poet whom he greatly admired. Virgil must have felt chagrined to show the author of Divina Commedia the suffering of Epicurus in the sixth circle of the inferno because, unlike Dante, Virgil was by most accounts a great

78

admirer of the character of Epicurus and his Garden
School.

During the period from the fourth century A.D.
until the late Renaissance Epicurus and his followers
were either "roasted," as in the vituperative writing
of Dante, or else ignored by scholars. Finally
in the seventeenth century in France and England
the Master was rediscovered and his ideas made an
important contribution to the literary temperament
of the times.

PIERRE GASSENDI AND THE REVIVAL

During the Renaissance a few thinkers: Lorenzo
Valla, Erasmus, Montaigne, and the Dominican Giordano
Bruno (who was burned at the stake by the Inquisition
in 1600 for his heretical beliefs) championed certain
principles from the school of the Garden. However,
it was not until a Roman Catholic priest, Pierre
Gassendi, began to write during the middle of the
seventeenth century that the modern Epicurean revival
started.

Gassendi, from Digne - a town in the foothills
of the French Alps, was a doctor of theology; a
canon and a provost in the cathedral church of his
home town. After teaching at the University of
Aix he began his study of the Master of the Garden.
For twenty years the priest worked on his studies
using primarily Diogenes Laertius and Lucretius
for his research. Finally in 1647 he published
a short treatise, Eight Books on the Life and Manners
of Epicurus. Hundreds of years before Gassendi
began his efforts to modify Epicurean ideas and
make them acceptable, another Roman Catholic
theologian, Thomas Aquinas, attempted to do a similar
adaptation of Greek philosophy to Christian theology.
Aquinas used Aristotle while Gassendi, who rejected
the Peripatetics, turned to the Garden.

The French priest devoted most of his life
to the study of atomism and Epicurean ethics.
Although he ran into opposition and much of his
writing was condemned by church authorities, Gassendi
became one of the most persuasive and important
thinkers of the century. His influence was

particularly great in England where he influenced such future philosophers as Hobbes and Locke.

EPICURUS AND THE RESTORATION

Shakespeare's The Tragedy of King Lear, written in 1606, has Goneril complaining to her father that "a hundred knights and squires" are so debauched and disorderly that they have made her home, ". . .like a riotous inn. Epicurism and lust make it more like a tavern or a brothel than a graced palace."[16] "Epicurism" in the early part of the seventeenth century was obviously a code word for dissolute, licentious living. Following the tradition from the early Christian era, the name of the leader of the Garden had entered the English language as a synonym for dissipation.

It was not until fifty years after Shakespeare wrote King Lear, and nine years after Gassendi published his treatise of a reappraisal of Epicurus in French, that a reassessment of the Greek teacher appeared in English. With the publication in 1656 of Epicurus's Morals, Walter Charleton began an era of Epicurean research which lasted until the early years of the eighteenth century. Between 1656 and 1700 at least thirteen books were published dealing with a new scholarly interpretation of Epicurus and Lucretius. The first and perhaps most significant of the works was Charleton's work.

WALTER CHARLETON

Walter Charleton, born in 1619, was educated at Oxford and became a noted medical doctor, eventually being chosen President of the English College of Physicians in 1689. He began his Epicurean studies after he was introduced to the work of Gassendi by Thomas Hobbes, the English philosopher who was a friend of the French priest. Charleton's publication on Epicurean ethics is written in the form of an essay paraphrasing the ideas he garnered from Diogenes Laertius, Lucretius, Seneca, Cicero, Plutarch and other writers. It is divided into thirty-one chapters, each averaging four pages in length, which deal with topics such as: pleasure, prudence, temperance, moderation, fortitude, justice, friendship and other Epicurean virtues. Considering the paucity of scholarship available at the time it remains an accurate evaluation of the Master's axiological position. Charleton was an excellent writer, he published over twenty-five books dealing with subjects ranging from anatomy to Stonehenge.

The most valuable part of his contribution to Epicurean studies is the preface to Epicurus's Morals in which he presents an eighteen page "Apologie" in defense of the Greek teacher. Charleton reflects, ". . . .as there is no Beauty without some moles, no chrystal (crystal) without some specks; so is not our EPICURUS without his imperfections. . . ."[17] Beginning with this caution the author develops his defense of the Master against the charges which, "incens'd the world against him." Using the three disputed principles, namely: opposition to immortality of the soul, opposition to worship and prayer to God, and advocacy of suicide in emergency, the English doctor shows that Epicurean ethics must be considered relative to the spirit of Hellenistic Athens. In addition, he argues that each of the popular charges against Epicurus is only partially true, and that other ancient writers can be accused of impiety and hedonism if their writings are taken out of context.

SIR WILLIAM TEMPLE

Few men of letters have had their reputations decline as precipitantly as the essayist Sir William Temple. Jonathan Swift, author of the classic Gulliver's Travels, mentioned in a memorial upon the death of Temple that he was universally recognized as the greatest writer of his age. Although few people recognize his name today, Temple had a large following when he wrote Upon the Gardens of Epicurus or, Of Gardening in 1685. The book was completed after the author had retired from an active political life in which he had served as a diplomat, adviser, and confidant to the English throne. Until his death in 1699, Temple lived the last eighteen years of his life following the prescripts of Epicurus in the gardens of Moor Park in Surrey, England.

81

The essay Upon the Gardens of Epicurus was an attempt to justify the "tranquillity of mind and indolence of body" which was at the heart of Epicurean philosophy. The word indolence to Temple meant freedom from pain, and this concept along with **ataraxia** he advocated as the panacea for unhappiness. Describing Epicurus as a philosopher with, ". . . .admirable wit, felicity of expression, excellence of nature, sweetness of conversation, temperance of life, and constancy of death. . . .,"[18] Temple shocked many of his contemporaries with his adulation for the pagan teacher. Not only did he approve of the Master, but his essay describes the Garden as an abode of happiness.

> The sweetness of air, the pleasantness of smells,
> the verdure of plants, the cleanness and lightness
> of food, the exercise of working and walking; but
> above all, the exemption from cares and solicitude
> seem equally to favour and improve both contemplation
> and health, the enjoyment of sense and imagination,
> and thereby the quiet and ease both of the body
> and mind.[19]

Temple in his exposition champions the joys of a retired life of quiet contemplation in an arbor of beauty; the essay represents a horticultural treatise with poetic overtones. The subject matter and style of writing reflects the love of rural life and the quiet joys of nature which have characterized the works of many writers, such as the Roman poet Horace and the American philosopher-naturalist Henry David Thoreau.

After Sir William Temple's effusive words of praise on the theme of **eudaemonia via ataraxia** in a scene of pastoral beauty, few additional seventeenth or eighteenth century writers touched on life and teachings in the Athenian Garden. One book, published by John Digby in London in 1712, proposed to offer "Epicurus' Morals with Comments and Reflections Taken out of Several Authors," however, this study misrepresents much of the Master's teaching. (Digby detested the notion that Epicurus advocated **Lathe Biosas**, so he attributes this aspect of Garden philosophy to Neocles, Epicurus' older brother.) Although inaccurate, with many philosophical premises on Epicureanism invented by the author rather than taken from historical sources, Digby, like Temple, helped popularize the ancient Greek teacher after

Epicurus had been so long-forgotten by history.

Unfortunately few scholarly books appeared on Epicurean studies after Temple and Digby. The Master was once again almost forgotten, only to be resurrected upon occasion through mention by an admirer. It is interesting that one such admirer is one of the most famous personages of American history.

AN EPICUREAN AMERICAN PRESIDENT

Surprisingly, for few historians acknowledge the fact, Thomas Jefferson declared himself a follower of the Master. On October 31, 1819 Jefferson wrote a letter to his good friend William Short in which he made his position very clear.

> As you say of yourself, I too am an Epicurean.
> I consider the genuine (not the imputed) doctrines
> of Epicurus as containing everything rational in
> moral philosophy which Greece and Rome have
> left us.[20]

In his letter Jefferson castigates the "incomprehensible Plato" and Stoics such as Epictetus and Cicero, who misrepresented the doctrines of Epicurus. Also the former President avows that he admires Jesus of Nazareth but finds difficulty in, "Abstracting what is really His from the rubbish in which it is buried. . . ."[21]

It is likely that such an affront to the Bible, should it have been made public at the time, would have been received with shocked indignation by some of Jefferson's pious Christian supporters. Fortunately in William Short he found a correspondent with whom he could freely trade ideas which he would never share with others or allow to be publicized to the general population.

Jefferson's letter to Short also contains an admonition that they should not let the Epicurean notion of tranquillity, which both men admired, cause "hebetude of mind." By this expression the famous statesman meant that **ataraxia** as a philosophy could, in the minds of some people, cause lethargy and indolence. In addition, Jefferson offered some Epicurean ideas in capsule form to his friend. These he entitled a "Syllabus of the Doctrines of Epicurus" and they included maxims of philosophy which were summarized from the extant works of the Greek philosopher.

During the long hiatus from Restoration England to the late Victorian era, little attention was given to Epicurus by scholars. It was not until the eighteen-eighties that two events occurred which sparked new attention to the old subject. The first incident happened in the Lycian city of Oenoanda in what is the present country of Turkey. The second occurrence was in Vatican City in Rome.

DIOGENES OF OENOANDA

In 1884 two Frenchmen discovered inscriptions carved into the walls of the market place of a small town in Asia Minor. During the second century A.D., when they were evidently carved, the inscriptions ran along a portico for as long as three hundred feet. Although broken by vandals and worn by age many of the stones have been deciphered to reveal an astonishing tribute to Epicureanism. During the years since their discovery, scholars have copied and translated the remains; offering insight into the testimonial of a fervent convert to the philosophy of the Garden.

The writer on the walls was a rich elderly Epicurean named Diogenes who wanted to record for posterity his appreciation of the Master's teaching. Diogenes of Oenoanda followed the Principal Doctrines in content so the remains offer little additional information on the ancient teaching, however, their discovery awakened interest in Epicureanism which was soon accelerated by another event.

CODEX VATICANUS

In 1888 C. Wotke discovered a fourteenth century manuscript in the Vatican. It contains the Meditations of Marcus Aurelius, the Moral Discourses of Epictetus and, most important, a collection of hitherto unknown maxims from Epicurean writings. Although some of the eighty-one quotations are from the Garden doctrines preserved by Diogenes Laertius, the remaining phrases represent a non-technical collection of moral theory offering new insight into Epicurean philosophy. The Codex Vaticanus (Vatican Collection) now provides scholars with information unavailable for earlier writers such as Gassendi, Charleton, Temple, and Digby.

At the same time the Vatican Collection was coming to the attention of the world of historical and philosophical research, Hermann Usener published his classic Epicurea. Usener collected all available citations from ancient sources about the Master and Garden teaching. Although never translated into English, Epicurea remains the definitive source for Epicurean quotations.

It was because of the Vatican Collection, the fragments from Oenoanda, and the work of Usener that the once forgotten and neglected Master of the Garden began to appear as the focus of numerous books and journal articles. Since the 1880's dozens of books and articles have appeared to resurrect the name of Epicurus and focus attention on a school which has influenced 2300 years of Western history. Once forgotten, Epicurus now offers a ripe crop for the scholar bent on gleaning a harvest of valuable historical evidence about life and education in ancient Greece.

EPICURUS TODAY

Epicureanism has been accused by modern commentators as being an "effeminate" philosophy because of its lack of assertiveness and confrontation with a changing and dynamic world. One author claims, "Persons of normal vitality are not attracted by it (Epicureanism); they are dubious of a standard that urges them to avoid human existence."[22] A famous twentieth century popularizer of history and philosophy, Will Durant, has proclaimed of the school, "The profoundest defect of the system is its negativity: it thinks of pleasure as freedom from pain, and of wisdom as an escape from the hazards and fullness of life; it provides an excellent design

85

for bachelorhood, but hardly for a society."[23]

Such charges, of course, could be made of many value systems and philosophies - most notably, Buddhism in the Eastern world and Schopenhauer's enlightened pessimism in the West. Because the philosophy of the Garden combines elements of Eastern quietism and Western materialism it may appear as an inconsistent axiology to some observers.

Unquestionably there is an element of escapism to Epicurus' **ataraxia**. Rejecting the noisy, competitive rat-race of society, adherents of the Garden philosophy are not swept by the rushing winds of change in a restless society. They are not caught in the continual acculturation to the new, the different; the fads and whims of a world racing to gratify its ceaseless craving for what is sometimes called progress.

Most Epicureans would agree with followers of the Buddha and Schopenhauer that assertiveness and confrontation with a dynamic world is Maya, an illusion - a joke fostered by our will (Schopenhauer) or our cravings and desires (Buddhism) to lead us into disaster. Only by rejecting the will and desires, by seeking permanence in the avoidance of pain and in the pleasure of tranquillity, can one break the cycle of anxiety which Epicurus said is the inheritance of most seekers-of-truth.

Schopenhauer stayed home in Frankfurt refusing to live in conformity to his neighbors, Buddhists quiet the mind by meditation on the transitory nature of reality, and Epicureans seek escape in friendship, mental stimulation, and serenity.

Seneca suggested that Epicurus was a hero disguised as a woman; he meant the Garden philosophy was reflective of feminine conduct: passivity, restraint, and quietness. Such sexist judgment appears naive, if not insulting, in today's age of sexual equality consciousness; yet, it is not an insult to accuse Epicureanism of exhibiting traits which exemplify ideals of peace, comfort, and security.

To Epicurus and his followers, from Greco-Roman to modern times, the world has offered continual threat to freedom from pain and mental serenity, and the only prudent life style offering succor

to the constant strife is retreat - retreat in a
society of friends ignoring the threat of equanimity
by familial fellowship in an environment of love,
dedicated to **eudaemonia via ataraxia**.

SYNOPSIS

The major purpose of this investigation of the educational work and school of Epicurus is to identify the most important features of an influential ancient philosophic system, which helped establish a model for Western education. The following are some of the conclusions which appear to be warranted by the findings of this study of Epicurus and his school:

1. Epicurus, often condemned as the philosopher of pleasure, led a personal life of asceticism. In his ethical conduct he exhibited the qualities of a saint by renouncing earthly rewards and physical pleasures to live abstemiously, dedicated to his axiological system.

2. By their life and teachings Epicurus and his associates served as examples in behavior for their students to emulate. Imitation of the life of a wise man was a significant educational methodological technique in the Garden School.

3. Gratitude in the form of veneration for teachers, similar to the attitude which characterized respect for saints and elders in the later Christian schools, was commonly exhibited by the Epicureans.

4. Teachers served **in loco parentis** by living with their students and sharing not only the educational climate, but the total social, physical, psychological, and emotional experiences of their pupils.

5. Faculty status in the Garden was based on a hierarchical order with associate leaders and assistant leaders serving under the direction of the head of the school. Much of the specific instruction was conducted by the assistant leaders while the associate leaders served as father-confessors and counselors to the students.

6. Much of the financial support for the Athenian Garden School was from donations offered by wealthy friends living in Mytilene, Lampsacus, and other areas outside of Attica. Such support was necessary because many of the students were impecunious and no tuition was charged for attendance at the school.

7. The Garden was one of the first boarding schools in antiquity. Similar to private boarding schools commonly found in Western society since the Reformation, Epicurus' institution offered a quiet retreat from the worldly affairs of the busy life of the city.

8. The philosophy of the Garden advanced the theory that private education, emphasizing the rights of the individual, took precedence over the needs of state. Epicurus anticipated the modern American theory of education in which each individual is recognized as worthy and unique; in which each student is encouraged to develop his interests and perfect his talents.

9. Similar to transcendentalist utopian educational communities and religious schools in modern America, such as the Amish, Epicurus' educational experiment sought seclusion from the worldly temptations of society. The Garden taught that students can only arrive at self-realization and discover the true source of happiness living in obscurity with congenial friends.

10. The Garden was a unique society exemplifying the present American public school policy of allowing all students, regardless of race, sex, creed, or national origin to study. Epicurus' Athenian school was the first in history to offer education without discrimination.

11. To the leader of the Garden, happiness was the sole aim of education. Using language similar to modern proponents of the theory of the open classroom and free school, Epicurus proclaimed that education should be an experience of pleasure and that joy in the classroom is a necessary ingredient to pedagogical success.

12. **Schole**, the word from which school is derived, was known to the Greeks as the leisurely pursuit of truth in serenity (**ataraxia**). Only one

90

ancient school realized the implications of this concept and taught in accordance with a policy of the theme: the Garden School.

13. To Epicurus the study of natural science was a necessary component in providing freedom from fear of the unknown. In this way, science served to refute myths and superstitions. The Garden was the first and only school in antiquity to dispel fantasies about the gods and monsters of legend.

14. Classical Greek education was rejected because Epicurus believed the traditional subjects would not contribute to **eudaemonia**. His school maintained that the educational and cultural adaptation taught at other schools avoided the crucial educational issue, that is, perfection of the mind in achieving **ataraxia**.

15. Empiricism and the dictates of reason became the methodological approach for instruction in the Garden. In addition, students were trained to use **phronesia**, prudence, as the guideline for exploring the world and achieving knowledge of the criteria of conduct most conducive to **eudaemonia**.

16. Garden teachings were dogmatic, particularly in the science and metaphysics of Epicurean philosophy. However, individual students were entrusted with the responsibility to cultivate an independent mind and use personal judgment when dealing with all matters of an axiological nature.

17. In the same way that holy books from the world's religions reveal doctrinal truth, the Epicurean students received revelation through the study of the Principal Doctrines and the memorization of dogma. Books were an important and effective means of popularizing the Master's tenets. In fact, the Garden could be described as a publishing house, perhaps the first in history.

18. Achievement of self-realization in the truth of Epicurean **eudaemonia** was the goal of each student. His progress in finding the happiness that results from peace of mind could not be evaluated by anyone other than himself. For this reason students marked their own progress in the Garden; appraisal of growth toward moral perfection was left to the individual.

19.   Frankness   and   candor   were   Epicurean
attributes   expressed   in   teaching   and   writing.   The
published   books,   reflecting   the   openness   of   speech
characterizing   all   teaching   in   the   Garden,   lacked
technical   language   and   pedantry.   Instead,   all
pronouncements by resident-members were clear, concise,
and easy to understand.

20.   To   the   Epicureans   friendship   was   proclaimed
as   the   greatest   boon   to   living   in   society.   **Philia**,
love   of   friendship,   became   the   vehicle   for   the
successful   cooperative   living   which   made   the   Garden
resemble one great family.

SOURCES OF QUOTATIONS

(Except where noted, translations were made by the author)

Preface:
[1]Benjamin Farrington, The Faith of Epicurus (London: Weidenfeld and Nicolson, 1967), p. 20.

Chapter I: EPICURUS THE TEACHER

[1]Epicurus Fragments: Fragments and Remains Assigned to Certain Books 30. (Cyril Bailey trans.).

[2]Epicurus Fragments: Vatican Collection XLVIII.

[3]Ibid.,XVII.

[4]Ibid., XLVII.

[5]Diogenes Laertius Lives of Eminent Philosophers: Epicurus X.6,7. (R. D. Hicks trans.).

[6]Lucius Annaeus Seneca Epistulae Morales XXI.10. (R. Gummere trans.).

[7]Epicurus Fragments and Remains 37.

[8]Ibid., 48.

[9]Seneca Epistulae Morales XI.8. (Gummere trans.).

[10]Ibid., XXV.5.

[11]Epicurus Fragments and Remains 31. (Bailey trans.)

[12]Titus Lucretius Carus De Rerum Natura III.7-14.

[13]Marcus Tullius Cicero De Finibus Bonorum Et Malorum V.1.3. (H. Rackham trans.).

Chapter II: THE EPICUREAN PHILOSOPHY OF HAPPINESS

[1]Epicurus Letter to Pythocles IV. 105b.   (Russel Geer trans.).

[2]Ibid., II.91.   (Geer trans.).

[3]Ibid., III.103b   (Geer trans.).

[4]Epicurus Principal Doctrines XI.   Festugiere-Chilton trans.).

[5]William Gerber, ed., The Mind of India (New York: Macmillan, 1967), p. XVII.

[6]Epicurus Letter to Menoeceus 128.

[7]Ibid., 129.   131.

[8]Ibid., 132.

[9]Seneca De Vita Beata XII.2.   (John Basore trans.).

[10]Epicurus Menoeceus 129.

[11]Ibid.

[12]Epicurus Doctrines IV.   (Norman Dewitt trans.).

[13]Epicurus Fragments: Usener 479.

[14]Ibid., 135.

[15]Epicurus Vatican Collection LXXXI.

[16]Epicurus Doctrines XXI.

[17]Epicurus Usener 551.

[18]Epicurus Doctrines XIV.

[19]Epicurus Vatican Collection LVIII.

[20]Epicurus Fragments and Remains 87.

[21]Seneca Epistulae Morales LXXIX.   15,16.   (Gummere trans.).

[22]Henry David Thoreau, Walden; Or, Life in the Woods

(London: Oxford University Press, 1910), p.5.

[23]Epicurus Fragments and Remains 68.

[24]Epicurus Usener 187.

[25]Ibid., 209.

[26]Thoreau, Walden, p. 5.

[27]Epicurus Vatican Collection XLI.

[28]Epictetus The Discourses as Reported by Arrian
III. vii. 19,21. (W. A. Oldfather trans.).

[29]Thoreau, Walden, p. 64.

[30]Diogenes Lives VI.121.

[31]Plutarch Moralia 778.c (Fowler trans.).

[32]Epicurus Vatican Collection LVI, LVII. (Bailey
trans.).

[33]Ibid., XXIII.

[34]Epicurus Doctrines XL.

[35]Ibid., XXVII.

[36]Seneca Epistulae Morales XIX. 10,11. (Gummere
trans.).

[37]Epicurus Vatican Collection XXVIII. (Festugiere-
Chilton trans.).

[38]Ibid., LII.

[39]Ibid., LXXVIII.

[40]Ibid., XVIII.

[41]Epicurus Fragments and Remains 33,34. (Bailey
trans.).

[42]Ibid., 32. (Bailey trans.).

Chapter III: THE GARDEN SCHOOL

[1] Epicurus _Menoeceus_ 122.

[2] Cicero _De Finibus_ I.xxi. 71,72. (Rackham trans.).

[3] Epicurus _Menoeceus_ 135.

[4] Cicero _De Finibus_ II.vii. 20. (Rackham trans.).

[5] Epicurus _Vatican Collection_ LXIV.

[6] _Ibid_., LXV.

[7] _Ibid_., LXXIX.

[8] Diogenes _Lives_ X. 118,119. (Hicks trans.).

[9] Epicurus _Doctrines_ V. (Geer trans.).

[10] Diogenes _Lives_ X. 138. (Hicks trans.).

[11] Epicurus _Doctrines_ XVI.

[12] Epicurus _Vatican Collection_ LXI. (Festugiere-
Chilton trans.).

[13] Diogenes _Lives_ X. 120. (Hicks trans.).

[14] _Ibid_., X. 118. (Hicks trans.).

[15] _Ibid_., X. 10. (Hicks trans.).

[16] Epicurus _Vatican Collection_ LXX.

[17] Diogenes _Lives_ X. 117. (Hicks trans.).

[18] Epicurus _Vatican Collection_ XXIX.

[19] _Ibid_., XXXVI. (Bailey trans.).

[20] Diogenes _Lives_ X. 9. (Hicks trans.).

[21] Epicurus _Usener_ 176. (Hicks trans.).

[22] Epicurus _Vatican Collection_ LXII. (Geer trans.).

[23] _Ibid_., LII.

[24]Ibid., LXXX.

Chapter IV: HISTORICAL COMMENT AND APPRAISAL

[1]Seneca De Otio III.2. (J. Basore trans.).

[2]Epictetus Encheiridion 12. (Oldfather trans.).

[3]Epicurus Usener 207.

[4]Epictetus Fragments II. (Carter trans.).

[5]Ibid., IV.iv. 10,11. (Oldfather trans.).

[6]Ibid, III.xiii. 11,12. (Oldfather trans.).

[7]Ibid., II.v. 2. (Thomas Gould trans.).

[8]Ecclesiastes 3:12,13. (New English Bible).

[9]Ibid., 5:10. (New English Bible).

[10]Ibid., 6:9. (New English Bible).

[11]Ibid., 8:15,16. (New English Bible).

[12]Ibid., 9:4,5. (New English Bible).

[13]Ibid., 11:10. (New English Bible).

[14]Ibid., 12:12. (New English Bible).

[15]Epicurus Vatican Collection XVII.

[16]Shakespeare King Lear I.iv. 265-267.

[17]Walter Charleton, Epicurus's Morals: Collected and Faithfully Englished "An Apologie for Epicurus," (London: Peter Davies, Publisher, 1926), [no page given].

[18]Sir William Temple, Five Miscellaneous Essays, ed. by Samuel Holt Monk (Ann Arbor: University of Michigan Press, 1963), pp. 7,8.

[19]Ibid., p. 10.

[20]Thomas Jefferson, The Life and Selected Writings of Thomas Jefferson, ed., by Adrienne Koch and William Peden (New York: Random House, 1944), p. 693.

[21]Ibid., p. 694.

[22]Julian L. Ross, Philosophy in Literature
(Syracuse: Syracuse University Press, 1949), p. 23.

[23]Will Durant The Story of Civilization: The Life
of Greece (New York: Simon & Schuster, 1939), p. 648.

SELECTED REFERENCES

1. Bailey, Cyril, The Greek Atomists and Epicurus.
   New York: Russell & Russell, Inc., 1928,
   pp. 34-529.

2. Barclay, William, "Hellenistic Thought in New
   Testament Times," The Expository Times,
   72:78-81, 101-104, 1960-61.

3. Bergson, Henri, The Philosophy of Poetry: The
   Genius of Lucretius. Translated by Wade
   Baskin. New York: The Philosophical
   Library, 1959, pp. 1-83.

4. Bonnard, Andre, Greek Civilization. Translated
   by R. C. Knight. London: George Allen and
   Unwin Ltd., 1961, pp. 259-281.

5. Charleton, Walter, Epicurus's Morals. London:
   Peter Davies, Publisher, 1926, pp. v-119.

6. Cicero, De Finibus Bonorum et Malorum.
   Translated by H. Rackham. The Loeb Classical
   Library. Cambridge: Harvard University
   Press, 1914, pp. 17-213.

7. DeLacy, P. H., "Lucretius and the History of
   Epicureanism," American Philosophical
   Association Transactions and Proceedings,
   79:12-23, 1948.

8. DeWitt, Norman W., "Organization and Procedure
   in Epicurean Groups," Classical Philology,
   31:205-211, July, 1936.

9. _____, "Epicurus' Three-Wheeled Chair," Classical
   Philology, 35:183-185, April, 1940.

10. _____, Epicurus and His Philosophy. Minneapolis:
    University of Minnesota Press, 1954, pp.
    Preface-377.

11. _____, St. Paul and Epicurus. Minneapolis:
    University of Minnesota Press, 1954, pp.4-195.

12. Digby, John, Life and Morals of Epicurus. London,
    England: J. Souter, 1822, pp. 1-167.

13. Elder, J. P., review of Epicurus and His
    Philosophy, by Norman Wentworth DeWitt,
    American Journal of Philology, 77:75-84,
    1956.

14. Epicurus, Epicurus the Extant Remains. Translated
    by Cyril Bailey. Oxford: Clarendon Press,
    1926, pp. 5-424.

15. _____, The Philosophy of Epicurus. Translated
    by George K. Strodach. Evanston, Illinois:
    Northwestern University Press, 1963, pp.
    v-255.

16. _____, Letters, Principal Doctrines, and Vatican
    Sayings. Translated by Russel M. Geer.
    The Library of Liberal Arts. New York:
    The Bobbs-Merrill Company, Inc., 1964,
    pp. v-92.

17. Farrington, Benjamin, Science and Politics in the
    Ancient World. New York: Barnes & Noble,
    Inc., 1939, pp. 118-233.

18. _____, The Faith of Epicurus. Weidenfeld Goldbacks.
    London: Weidenfeld and Nicolson, 1967,
    pp. xi-153.

19. Festugiere, A. J., Epicurus and His Gods. Trans-
    lated by C. W. Chilton. New York: Russell
    & Russell, 1955, pp. vii-96.

20. Fite, Warner, An Adventure in Moral Philosophy.
    London: Methuen & Co., Ltd., 1926, pp. 170-
    192.

21. Freeman, Kathleen, "Epicurus - A Social Experiment,"
    Greece and Rome, 7:156-168, May, 1938.

22. Gassendi, Pierre, The Selected Works of Pierre
    Gassendi. Edited and translated by Craig
    B. Bruch. New York: Johnson Reprint
    Corporation, 1972, pp. viii, 380-392.

23. Glidden, David Kenneth, The Epicurean Theory of
     Knowledge. Unpublished Doctoral Dissertation,
     Princeton, New Jersey: Princeton University,
     1971, pp. 1-291.

24. Hibler, Richard W., "Epicurus and His Garden
     School," The History Teacher (Queensland,
     Australia), 18:27-42, October 1976.

25. _____,"Thoreau and Epicurus," The Thoreau Society
     Bulletin, 129:1-3, Fall, 1974.

26. Hicks, R. D., Stoic and Epicurean. New York:
     Russell & Russell, Inc., 1962, pp. 153-312.

27. Landor, Walter Savage, Imaginary Conversations
     and Poems. London: J.M. Dent and Sons,
     1933, pp. 118-144.

28. Laertius, Diogenes, Lives of Eminent Philosophers
     Vol. II. Translated by R. D. Hicks. The
     Loeb Classical Library. Cambridge: Harvard
     University Press, 1925, pp. 529-677.

29. Lucretius, Lucretius on the Nature of Things
     [De Rerum Natura]. Translated by Cyril
     Bailey. Oxford: Clarendon Press, 1910,
     pp. 5-311.

30. _____,The Way Things Are [De Rerum Natura].
     Translated by Rolfe Humphries. Bloomington:
     Indiana University Press, 1968, pp.7-255.

31. Mayo, Thomas F., Epicurus in England 1650-1725.
     Dallas, Texas: Southwest Press, 1934, pp.
     xi-209.

32. Merlan, Philip, Studies in Epicurus and Aristotle.
     Weisbaden, West Germany: Otto Harrassowitz,
     1960, pp. 12-37.

33. Panichas, George A., Epicurus. New York: Twayne
     Publishers, Inc., pp. Preface-173.

34. Pater, Walter, Marius the Epicurean. A Signet
     Classic. New York. New American Library,
     1970, pp. 239-256.

35. Plutarch, Moralia. Vol. XIV. Translated by
     Einarson and DeLacy. The Loeb Classical

Library. Cambridge: Harvard University Press, 1967, p. 3-13, 153-173.

36. Poulsen, Frederik, Fra Epikurs Have. Kobenhavn: Boghallen, 1948, pp. 7-43.

37. Radin, Max, Epicurus My Master. Chapel Hill: The University of North Carolina Press, 1949, pp. 125-135.

38. Richter, Gisela M. A., The Portraits of the Greeks. Vol. II. London: The Phaidon Press, Ltd., 1965, pp. 108-120.

39. Rist, J. M., Epicurus an Introduction. Cambridge University Press, 1972, pp. 1-185.

40. Saint-Evremond, Charles de Marquetel, Seigneur de, The Letters of Saint Evremond. Edited by John Hayward. London: George Routledge and Sons, 1930, pp. 273-280.

41. Santayana, George, Three Philosophical Poets. Double-Anchor Books. Garden City, New York: Doubleday & Company, Inc., 1910, pp. 11-70.

42. Sedgwick, Henry Dwight, The Art of Happiness of the Teachings of Epicurus. Freeport, New York: Books for Libraries Press, 1933, pp. ix-181.

43. Seneca, Epictulae Morales I Books I-LXV. Translated by R. M. Gummere. The Loeb Classical Library. Cambridge: Harvard University Press, 1917, pp. 3-149.

44. _____, Moral Essays II. Translated by J. W. Basore. The Loeb Classical Library. Cambridge: Harvard University Press, 1932, pp. 99-285.

45. Smith, Martin F., "New Fragments of Diogenes of Oenoanda," American Journal of Archaeology, 75:357-389, 1971.

46. Taylor, Alfred Edward, Epicurus. Freeport, New York: Books for Libraries Press, 1911, pp. v-122.

47. Temple, Sir William, Five Miscellaneous Essays.

Edited by Samuel Holt Monk. Ann Arbor: The
University of Michigan Press, 1963, pp.
vii-36.

48. Wallace, William, Epicureanism. London: Society
for Promoting Christian Knowledge, 1880,
pp. 1-170.

49. Wright, Frances, A Few Days in Athens. New York:
Peter Eckler, Publisher, [no date], pp. v-159.

50. Zeller, Euard, The Stoics, Epicureans and Sceptics.
Translated by Oswald J. Reichel. New York:
Russell & Russell, Inc., 1962, pp. 404-514.

ABOUT THE AUTHOR

Dr. Richard W. Hibler holds degrees from Bethany College (W. Va.), Michigan State University, and The University of Wyoming. He is currently Professor of Education in the School of Professional Studies at the State University of New York, College at Potsdam. Dr. Hibler's publications have appeared in journals in Great Britain, West Germany, Canada, Australia, and the United States.